THE CONSTITUTION OF *Selves*

THE CONSTITUTION

Cornell University Press

O F *Selves*

Marya Schechtman

ITHACA AND LONDON

First published 1996 by Cornell University Press.
First printing, Cornell Paperbacks, 2007
Library of Congress Cataloging-in-Publication Data
Schechtman, Marya, 1960–
    The constitution of selves / Marya Schechtman.
        p.   cm.
    Includes bibliographical references and index.
    ISBN 978-0-8014-7417-0
    1. Identity.   2. Self.   3. Self-knowledge, Theory of.
    4. Individuality.   I. Title.
    BC199.I4S33   1996
    126—dc20   96-16537

Printed in the United States of America

This book is printed on Lyons Falls Turin Book,
a paper that is totally chlorine-free and acid-free.

Contents

Preface

The personal identity problem has enjoyed a revival among analytic philosophers over the last three decades. Since questions of personal identity are of fundamental interest outside philosophy, there is some reason to hope that in this area philosophy will do what it is popularly thought to do—apply rigorous standards of argument and investigation to basic problems of human existence. A glance at the contemporary literature on personal identity, however, quickly disappoints these expectations. Instead of questions of self-knowledge, self-expression, and authenticity, we find discussions of the necessary and sufficient connections between entities called individual "person time-slices" which allow us to say they are slices of the same person. These creatures inhabiting philosophical theories of identity seem to have little to do with persons as we know them, and the concerns about identity these theorists address seem far removed from the compelling identity issues familiar to us from lived experience, psychology, and literature.

The contemporary philosophical discussion of identity omits a great deal that seems central to the topic of personal identity. This book is motivated by my own disappointment. My goal is to articulate more clearly what contemporary analytic work on personal identity neglects. In Part I, I consider central issues from within the contemporary debate, arguing that current analytic identity theorists have failed even on their own terms. In Part II, I step outside the confines of standard personal identity literature, using resources and issues neglected by the standard discussion to provide more robust and satisfying perspectives on questions about persons and personal identity. Here I focus on our experience of life as lived history, investigating how personal identity is linked to the capacity to construct coherent autobiographical narratives and to enter into the activities and social interactions that define the lives of persons.

Much of the preliminary work involved in understanding and criticizing the standard debate on personal identity got under way at Harvard University. I am grateful to the many friends and teachers there who guided me through the preliminary phases and have continued to provide support, insight, and inspiration. First and foremost, I thank Stanley Cavell, who helped shape my most basic sensibilities by demonstrating exciting new ways to engage with traditional philosophical debates. His influence can be felt on every page of the book. I also thank Burton Dreben, Juliet Floyd, Sharon Lloyd, Nick Pappas, Hilary Putnam, Tim Scanlon, Miriam Solomon, and Paul Weithman, each of whom made a crucial contribution to my project in one way or another, and Jennifer Whiting, who gave me my first systematic introduction to the topic of personal identity. I also thank Harvard for generous financial support and the Woodrow Wilson Fellowship Foundation for granting me a Charlotte Newcombe Dissertation Fellowship for the academic year 1987–88.

I wrote the bulk of this book while on the faculty at The University of Illinois at Chicago. The philosophy department there is an extraordinarily congenial place to work; I can hardly imagine a department more nurturing of its faculty. I am deeply grateful to my colleagues—past and present—for their generosity with everything: leaves of absence, scheduling flexibility, encouragement, and time spent reading and commenting on work in progress. I especially thank Charles Chastain, Walter Edelberg, Dorothy Grover, Bill Hart, Christopher Hoyt, Peter Hylton, Connie Meinwald, Paul Teller, and Kent Wilson for their insights, suggestions, and enthusiasm. I also thank the university for its support and for a Campus Research Board grant that freed me from teaching duties in the spring of 1990.

Many others have also played central roles in the completion of my project. Here I acknowledge two especially important debts. Randy Carter's comments on the manuscript were always clear and valuable. In addition, he led me to a body of literature that together with his suggestions resulted in a total reconfiguration of Part I. Richard Wollheim has had an impact on the project since its inception. His book *The Thread of Life*, which came out while I was just beginning my work on personal identity, gave me the courage to pursue my intuitions and a rich set of resources to employ while doing so. Not only have his views continued to have a major impact on the formation of my own, but his gracious critique helped me to sharpen and focus the argument of Part II.

The manuscript was also vastly improved by the suggestions and comments of an enormously sympathetic and insightful referee at Cornell University Press, and by the extremely helpful input of my editor, Roger Haydon.

Finally, I thank my family and my husband, John Marko, whose conversation, enthusiasm for my work, and overall support have been essential to the preparation of this book.

MARYA SCHECHTMAN

New York City

The Constitution of Selves

Introduction

Facts about personal identity stand at the core of our ordinary practice and lay the foundations for our day-to-day interactions. Philosophical problems of identity should thus be compelling, accessible, and of general appeal. Yet treatments of this topic in contemporary analytic philosophy have been highly abstract, technical, and specialized. Philosophical discussion has yielded some extremely sophisticated theories of personal identity, but they do not seem to be about persons as we know them, nor do they capture the real-world implications of personal identity. Indeed, it has been notoriously difficult for any of the views of identity currently in vogue to explain why personal identity matters to us at all.

It may be an unfortunate fact that treating real-life concerns with philosophical rigor necessarily robs them of some of their pre-philosophical interest. Still, debates about personal identity have become so far removed from the concerns that originally impelled them that it seems as if something more must be amiss in this case. In what follows I argue that the problem with philosophical accounts of personal identity originates in the failure of contemporary identity theorists to recognize the full complexity of the issues they discuss. These theorists do not recognize that there is no monolithic "question of personal identity," but rather a variety of identity questions arising in different contexts, bearing diverse significance, and demanding distinct kinds of answers. It is thus important for philosophers working on the topic of personal identity to be clear about which question of identity is under consideration. Failure to achieve such clarity confuses the discussion in a way that impedes progress on *any* identity question.

This book uncovers and addresses an especially significant and philosophically costly example of this phenomenon. Most modern personal identity theorists, I charge, conflate two significantly different questions, which I call the reidentification question and the characterization question. The former is the question of what makes a person at time t_2 the same person as a person at time t_i; the latter the question of which beliefs, values, desires, and other psychological features make someone the person she is. The reidentification question thus concerns the logical relation of identity, whereas the characterization question concerns identity in the sense of what is generally called, following Erikson, an "identity crisis."

Those working on what is called "the problem of personal identity" in the modern English-speaking tradition usually address themselves formally to the reidentification question and so expect their views to take the form of a reidentification criterion. I maintain that these "reidentification theorists" fail to appreciate the boundaries of this question. As a result considerations linked to the characterization question creep into their investigation and are used (inappropriately) to guide their formulation of reidentification criteria, which undermines their project (as currently conceived) at its very foundations.

The fatal confusion stems from the central role reidentification theorists give to the practical importance of personal identity. There is a strong pre-philosophical sense that facts about identity underlie facts about four basic features of personal existence: survival, moral responsibility, self-interested concern, and compensation (hereafter "the four features"). That we have such an intuition, and that it stands at the core of many of our basic practices, is beyond question. Reidentification theorists seem to assume that since they are working on defining personal identity, and since identity is linked to the four features, their definition of identity must capture that link. They thus use the ability to make sense of the connection between the four features and personal identity as a test of the acceptability of proposed reidentification criteria.

It is the use of this constraint which leads contemporary theorists into trouble. I contend that the four features are indeed linked to facts about personal identity, but identity in the sense at issue in the characterization question, not the reidentification question. It is thus a theory of characterization and not of reidentification that is properly charged with the responsibility of explaining the connection between identity and the four features. The attempt to make a reidentification criterion do so is thus out of place and, in the end, doomed to failure. Because reidentification theorists do not recognize this, they are forced into contortions that render them incapable of capturing our intuitions about either the four features or reidentification.

In order to push the discussion of personal identity forward it is necessary to separate the two questions and deal with each in its own terms. The reidentification question must be pursued without the unreasonable demand that it speak to our intuitions about the four features, and the four features must be investigated within the more congenial context of the characterization question, where they belong. In what follows I argue for this claim and offer an account of characterization that explains the intuitive link between identity and the four features.

This book advances the discussion of personal identity in several ways. Most generally, it shows how the conflation of different identity questions can undermine useful discussion and so underscores the need to recognize the multifarious nature of personal identity and keep clear on exactly which question is under consideration. Second, it frees reidentification theories from the futile attempt to capture the link between identity and the four features, thus making it possible to pursue the reidentification question productively (a task I do not undertake, but whose general contours I do discuss). Finally, it provides a positive view of characterization, offering insight into one of the most compelling questions of personal identity and shedding light on the relation between personal identity and survival, moral responsibility, self-interested concern, and compensation.

Part I

Reidentification

1

The Reidentification Question

Contemporary philosophers of personal identity in the analytic tradition place their concern about personal identity within the context of more general worries about the identity conditions of changing objects over time—the ship of Theseus is replaced plank by plank, the acorn becomes a mighty oak, and persons change both physically and psychologically. The general problem then is the metaphysical question of how a single entity persists through change. The more specific question is the question of how a single person does. In this chapter I outline some of the most basic features of this investigation—its goals and the strongest theory it produces. In the next two chapters I show that this theory is constitutionally incapable of capturing our concerns about the importance of identity.

Reidentification Criteria

Put most simply, the goal of contemporary personal identity theorists is to provide a criterion of personal identity over time. A criterion of personal identity could either be a means by which we in fact make judgments of identity (in John Perry's terms, a "way of knowing," in Derek Parfit's, "our way of telling whether some present object is identical with some past object")[1] or, alternatively, a specification of the necessary and sufficient conditions for identity (in Perry's terms, the "unity relations between . . . nonsimultaneous person-stages," in Parfit's, "*what this identity necessarily involves, or consists in*").[2]

The goal of personal identity theorists is to offer a criterion of the latter sort. Their question is metaphysical, not epistemological; they want to tell

[1]John Perry, "Introduction," in Perry, ed., *Personal Identity* (Berkeley and Los Angeles: University of California Press, 1976), p. 11; Derek Parfit, *Reasons and Persons* (Oxford: Clarendon Press, 1984), pp. 202–3.
[2]Perry, "Introduction," p. 11; Parfit, *Reasons and Persons*, p. 203.

us not just how we *know* when we have one and the same person at two different times, but what *makes* someone the same person at those two times. This distinction, and the attitude of contemporary theorists, is nicely summed up by Harold Noonan:

> The problem of personal identity over time is the problem of giving an account of the logically necessary and sufficient conditions for a person identified at one time being the same person as a person identified at another. Otherwise put, it is the problem of giving an account of what personal identity over time necessarily consists in, or, as many philosophers phrase it, the problem of specifying the criterion of personal identity over time. On an alternative use of the term 'criterion', to specify a criterion of personal identity over time would be to say something about what could count as evidence for personal identity. It is important to be aware at the outset that this is *not* what philosophers are interested in when they debate the problem of personal identity. Their concern is with the constitutive, the metaphysical-cum-semantic, not the evidential, criterion of personal identity.[3]

Whatever criterion reidentification theorists offer, then, it must do more than simply provide a means of determining whether a person at time t_2 is the same person as a person at time t_1; it must tell us what it *is* for him to be the same person.

In light of this goal reidentification theorists need a way to define a person at t_2 and a person at t_1 without knowing whether they are the same person. This is easy enough; they simply confine their attention to particular temporal segments of a person's life, and the reidentification question is taken to be the question of what relation these segments must bear to one another to be part of the life of the same person. The problem of personal identity is thus generally described as the problem of determining what relation must hold between two "person-stages" (or "person time-slices"—I use the terms interchangeably) to make them stages or slices of the same person. This statement of the question is common, but there is disagreement worth discussing about exactly how time-slices are to be conceived.

There is, first of all, the question of their duration. It is not obvious whether we are to think of time-slices as instantaneous cross sections of a person's history or as having some brief duration. There seems to be some equivocation between the two positions in the literature. In general, these time-slices are described as momentary (both David Lewis and Sydney

---

[3]Harold Noonan, *Personal Identity* (London: Routledge, 1991), p. 2.

Shoemaker, who in other respects hold very different views, talk about momentary stages).[4] There is, however, a problem with this description: person-stages are also supposed to be recognizable as stages of persons, and so are supposed to be subjects; that is, they are supposed to take actions and have beliefs, desires, goals, intentions, and so on. Lewis tells us that a person-stage "does many of the same things that a person does; it talks and walks and thinks, it has beliefs and desires, it has a size and shape and location. It even has a temporal duration. But only a brief one, for it does not last long."[5] And Noonan draws the implications from this claim, saying, "It might be hard to deny that person-stages *are* persons. For they walk and talk and think, and have beliefs and desires. What more could one ask? . . . It is clear . . . that such a person-stage, existing on its own, and not as a proper part of a larger aggregate of person-stages, will be a person."[6]

The tension is obvious. Beliefs, values, desires, intentions, actions, and characteristics are things that cannot take place in an instant. A literal instant is not even long enough to experience something as basic as pleasure or pain; it is not long enough to see an afterimage, or hear a tone—let alone be loyal, have doubts about one's religion, or be moody or consistent. Lewis is sensitive to this. He says "a stage cannot do everything that a person can do, for it cannot do those things that a person does over a longish interval."[7] Still, I do not think he confronts the full implications of this fact, which are more extreme than he seems to realize. To do *any* of the things that are recognizable as the activities of persons, a person-stage must endure for at least several seconds. To have some rich enough complement of characteristics to be anything like a *"person* identified at a time," a person time-slice probably has to last at least several minutes, perhaps even much longer. If, then, we want to build a criterion of identity over time by identifying distinct temporal stages as stages of the same person, these stages have to endure long enough for them to be person-like in their characteristics.

This seems to settle the issue. We should take the talk about momentary or instantaneous stages with a grain of salt and think instead of stages as having some brief duration. This approach, however, is also problematic because it interferes with the goal of philosophical identity theorists. If what

[4]David Lewis, "Survival and Identity," in *Philosophical Papers*, vol. 1 (Oxford: Oxford University Press, 1983), p. 58; Sydney Shoemaker, "A Materialist's Account," in Shoemaker and Richard Swinburne, *Personal Identity* (Oxford: Blackwell, 1984), p. 75.
[5]Lewis, "Survival and Identity," p. 76.
[6]Noonan, *Personal Identity*, p. 126.
[7]Lewis, "Survival and Identity," p. 76.

the reidentification theorist is really interested in doing is providing an analysis of *what it is* for a person to persist over time, then employing person-stages of some duration prevents the criterion from being general enough. Suppose, for instance, that we use the reidentification criterion to tell us what makes a person at age eleven (that is, the stage from her eleventh birthday to her twelfth) the same person as the person at age forty (that is, from her fortieth birthday to her forty-first). Here the person-stages last a year, and there is no problem yet. If, however, we are to have a general criterion of identity over time, it should also be able to tell us what makes the person on her fortieth birthday (a stage of one day) the same person as the person on her forty-first birthday; and what makes the person from noon to one on her fortieth birthday the same person as the person from five to six on her fortieth birthday, and so on. The limiting case is clear. If a criterion of reidentification for persons over time is really meant to be a general analysis of what is necessary and sufficient to identify two "persons" (or person-stages) at two times as the same person, then it should be able to tell us what makes a person at one instant the same person as a person at *any* other time—even the next instant. If this is to be done in terms of person-stages or time-slices, these must be conceived of as instantaneous.

It is easy to miss this tension because philosophical discussion of personal identity tends to shift back and forth without announcement between our everyday interests in reidentifying persons and the philosopher's specialized interest in providing a definition of personal identity over time. Our ordinary concerns about reidentification are virtually never about identity from instant to instant, but over much larger periods of time. When we are asking these questions, we are thus usually trying to identify large temporal segments of persons with one another, and so the claim that the time-slices that are being identified are themselves person-like subjects sounds plausible. In philosophical discourse, however, where the stated goal is to provide an account of what constitutes the continuation of a person, we need an account of identity over the course of extended temporal segments of persons' lives as well as over their entire lives—and this requires instantaneous time-slices. I am not sure how this tension should be resolved, nor have I ever seen anyone address it directly. I return to it in later chapters, but for now it is important to see that it exists and to note that it suggests that the problem addressed by reidentification theorists is somewhat different from our ordinary problems of reidentifying persons.

A second controversy about time-slices has to do with the question of what they are slices of—persons, or the lives of persons. This controversy establishes the distinction between those who view persons as four-dimensional, and those who see them as enduring three-dimensional objects (or between those who think persons endure and those who think they perdure, or between those who subscribe to the Doctrine of Temporal Parts and those who do not, or any of the many other terminologies that have been used to express these alternatives).

The relevant distinction here is nicely described by Shoemaker, who rejects the four-dimensionalist view. He tells us that some philosophers who talk about person-stages

> think of persons and other continuants as four-dimensional objects which have temporal as well as spatial parts. For them momentary stages will be either temporally very small parts of continuants or temporally unextended cross-sections of them taken at particular moments of time. But one need not be committed to the four-dimensional view of ordinary continuants in order to use this terminology. Person-stages can be thought of as 'temporal slices', not of persons, but of the histories or careers of persons.[8]

Those who believe persons are three-dimensional enduring objects thus believe that a person is wholly present at each time in his history, and time-slices of that history are not to be viewed as genuine *parts* of a person. Those who believe that persons are four-dimensional perduring objects believe that a person is never wholly present at any one time, but only over time, and that person-stages are parts out of which continuant persons are composed.[9]

A final debate surrounding time-slices has to do with their ontological status. The question is whether they have ontological priority over continuant persons (the reductionist view of persons) or whether they are themselves parasitic on the notion of continuant persons (the nonreductionist view of persons). The reductionist believes that time-slices are the more fundamental entities and that persons are secondary, or derivative, constructs of time-slices. Nonreductionists, on the other hand, give time-slices no such priority.

A prime example of the reductionist point of view is found in Parfit's work. Having laid out the two views he takes to be the prime candidates for a theory of personal identity, he tells us that they

---

[8]Shoemaker, "A Materialist's Account," p. 75.

[9]The disagreement about whether persons are three-dimensional or four-dimensional is part of the debate about whether continuant objects in general are three-dimensional or four-dimensional. This controversy plays a central role in my later argument against reidentification theorists. Here, however, I want only to introduce it.

are both *Reductionist*. They are Reductionist because they claim
> (1) That the fact of a person's identity over time just consists in the holding of certain more particular facts,

and
> (2) that these facts can be described without either presupposing the identity of this person, or explicitly claiming that the experiences in this person's life are had by this person, or even explicitly claiming that this person exists. These facts can be described in an *impersonal* way.[10]

In short, if persons are constructed from time-slices, then the world can be completely described without any mention of persons.

An example of the nonreductionist view is to be found in the work of Shoemaker, who tells us that to him "it is quite obvious that the conceptually prior notion is that of a person, not that of a momentary person-stage or experience."[11] Lewis also claims to hold a nonreductionist view of persons. Although he says that "a continuant person is an aggregate of person-stages," he later tells us that when he says this he does "*not* claim to be reducing 'constructs' to 'more basic' entities."[12] In the end, I believe, it may not be as easy to be both a four-dimensionalist and a nonreductionist as Lewis asserts.

As a final note on this dispute, I point out that even a nonreductionist must give time-slices a certain amount of independence from the person *of whom they are slices*. A nonreductionist reidentification theorist can hold that a person time-slice is not definable without reference to continuant persons, but it had better be definable without reference to the person of whom it is a part, or the reidentification theory will be viciously circular. If the only way one can define a person-stage is in terms of the identity of the person of whom it is a stage, then a criterion of identity based on relations between time-slices is singularly uninformative. Reidentification theorists of any sort are thus committed to at least this weak form of reductionism.

Bearing in mind these controversies of interpretation, we can now offer a general characterization of the reidentification theorists' goal as that of providing a criterion of personal identity that defines the necessary and sufficient conditions for saying that a person-stage at t_2 and a person-stage at t_1 are stages of the same person.

---

[10]Parfit, *Reasons and Persons*, p. 210.
[11]Shoemaker, "A Materialist's Account," p. 101.
[12]Lewis, "Survival and Identity," p. 22, and *Philosophical Papers*, p. 177.

Arguments for the Psychological Continuity Theory

We have seen the general form of the question reidentification theorists ask and the form they expect a response to that question to take. In addition, of course, it is at least a preliminary requirement that whatever theory of personal identity we accept capture our pre-philosophical conception of that relation.[13] Reidentification theorists take themselves to be addressing *the* fundamental philosophical problem of personal identity and so assume that an acceptable criterion of personal identity should be able to capture *all* of our most basic intuitions. This has led to one of the most intractable debates in the literature—that between those who believe that personal identity should be defined in terms of the continuation of a single human body or part thereof (the bodily continuity theory) and those who believe that it should be defined in terms of the continuation of a single psychological life (the psychological continuity theory).[14]

The pull of the bodily continuity theory is probably more immediately evident than that of the psychological continuity theory. We do tend to make judgments of identity on this basis. This is true both in informal cases (for example, I recognize my friend by looking at him, I know that Aunt Bessie was at the reunion when she shows me a snapshot depicting her body at the festivities), and in cases of dispute (for example, I show that I am the depositor of the funds by showing a photo ID, it is proved that the defendant really is the criminal through fingerprinting and genetic testing, I know that one twin is posing as the other by noting the telltale birthmark). Evidence that the present human body is the same as the past one is thus implicitly accepted as evidence that the present *person* is the same as the past one. This basic intuition has been developed into a variety of different versions of the bodily continuity theory—ranging from the view that most of the human being must continue, through the view that the brain must continue, to the view that enough of the brain to be the brain of a living person must continue. All of these see a physical basis for personal identity.

---

[13] I should say at the outset that I do not believe that any single view can capture all such intuitions. This is because, as I said in the introduction, I believe that we have a great many different concerns about persons that issue in different kinds of questions, requiring different kinds of answers.

[14] Historically there is a third option—the view that personal identity over time consists in the continuation of the same immaterial soul. I do not discuss this possibility in much detail because it is widely believed to have been discredited and is not a major part of the current discussion. I do refer to it where relevant.

There is, however, another set of intuitions about persons which seems to pull us away from the bodily continuity theory. It is a fundamental feature of persons that facts about their identities have deeply significant practical implications. These facts play an absolutely basic role in our day-to-day lives. In what follows, I focus on four of the most representative and widely discussed aspects of importance that attach to facts about personal identity: moral responsibility, self-interested concern, compensation, and survival (the "four features" identified in the introduction).

We believe, first of all, that facts about personal identity are crucial in determining facts about moral responsibility—a person can only be held responsible for her own actions.[15] We also feel that there is a particular *kind* of interest that it is rational to have in one's own future. Although we may care as *much* about others as about ourselves, there is a *type* of interest one properly has only for oneself.[16] Because of this self-interest, facts about compensatory fairness are also linked to facts about identity. A person is only compensated for his sacrifices by benefits that accrue to *him*.[17]

Perhaps most central of all, however, is the link between personal identity and survival. In ordinary circumstances the question of whether or not one will continue to exist cannot be a matter of indifference. As John Perry puts it in a particularly graphic example, "You learn that someone will be run

---

[15]We can imagine, I suppose, cases that seem to contradict this: parents may be held responsible for their children's actions, or a person may be held responsible for the action of someone else if she somehow brought it about (for example, if I yell "fire" in a crowded theater I may be responsible for the injuries in the stampede or the emptying of the fire extinguisher by a zealous employee). If we are talking about our ordinary moral conceptions, however, and not the law, these cases do not really pose a counterexample to my claim. In each case we are holding the person responsible for actions that result from his prior actions, and so the assignment of responsibility for someone else's actions is always via a more primary ascription of another action to the person who is being held responsible. I think it is safe to say that in general it is part of our ordinary conception of both persons and moral responsibility that persons can be appropriately held responsible only for their own actions.

[16]I have a great deal to say about the nature of this special self-interested concern in later chapters. For now, however, it can be best distinguished from our concern for others by the fact that it is based on anticipation. I expect to *feel* my own experiences and so care in a special way about their character. For a nice discussion of the characteristics defining self-interested concern and how it differs from our concern for others, see Richard Wollheim, *The Thread of Life* (Cambridge: Harvard University Press, 1984), pp. 236–56.

[17]Once again, there is an apparent counterexample to this claim. I can, of course, be compensated by benefits to others if these also benefit me. The sacrifice I make smiling by my spouse's side during his campaign can, for instance, be rewarded by his being elected, but that is because I want him to be elected, either for the material rewards it will bring me, or because I love him and seeing him happy in turn makes me happy. The point, however, is that in such cases *I* do receive rewards *through* the rewards to someone else.

over by a truck tomorrow; you are saddened, feel pity, and think reflectively about the frailty of life; one bit of information is added, that the someone is you, and a whole new set of emotions rise in your breast."[18] The belief that one will not survive some ordeal is likely to engender terror, depression, and in some cases, perhaps, even relief. Only in the most unusual of circumstances, however, can consideration of this possibility be met with total apathy. All of this affect attaches directly to facts about personal identity, for these seem to determine facts about survival—I care deeply about whether or not *I* will still be around in the future.[19]

It is beyond doubt that facts about identity *are* important to us. A theory of personal identity should thus make sense of this; the relation that defines identity should be important in the ways identity is. It is this demand which is the basis for the claim that personal identity must be defined in terms of psychological rather than bodily continuity. This is not obvious, nor is it how arguments for the psychological continuity theory are usually described. A close look at those arguments shows, however, that it is our sense of the practical importance of identity that drives them.

To see this we need to have a clearer sense of what the arguments for the psychological continuity theory are. These arguments almost always take the form of hypothetical cases in which we are asked to imagine the separation of bodily continuity from psychological continuity and then make judgments concerning personal identity. It is assumed that we will judge that the person goes with the psychological life rather than with the body. Psychological continuity theorists thus argue that personal identity must consist in psychological continuity. They explain that because bodily continuity and psychological continuity usually go together, bodily continuity provides good *evidence* for personal identity. However, they continue, our reactions to the cases in which we imagine a separation of the two types of continuity shows that it is psychological continuity that really underlies identity.

A closer look at the hypothetical cases used to argue for the psychological continuity theory bears out my claim that the support for this view comes from our beliefs about identity and survival, moral responsibility, self-interested concern, and compensation. The argument that personal identity must be defined in psychological terms is first systematically presented and defended by Locke in his *Essay concerning Human Understanding*. There Locke argues that "*personal identity* consists, not in the Identity of Sub-

[18]John Perry, "The Importance of Being Identical," in A. Rorty, ed., *The Identities of Persons* (Berkeley and Los Angeles: University of California Press, 1976), p. 67.
[19]Derek Parfit challenges this claim. I discuss Parfit's position in Chapter 2.

stance, but . . . in the Identity of *consciousness*."[20] Locke uses a number of cases to show that sameness of body and/or immaterial soul (the soul being construed as featureless immaterial substance) is irrelevant to the continued existence of the same person—sameness of either kind of substance being neither necessary nor sufficient for personal identity.

He argues that sameness of body is not *necessary* to sameness of person by asking us to imagine, for instance, the consciousness of a prince inhabiting the body of a cobbler. He says, "Everyone sees, he would be the same Person with the Prince, *accountable* only for the Prince's Actions."[21] He argues that sameness of body is not *sufficient* for sameness of person by asking us to imagine someone who has the same immaterial substance as Nestor or Thersites at the Battle of Troy, but with no consciousness of their actions, and asks, "Can he be *concerned* in either of their Actions? Attribute them to himself, or think them his own more than the Actions of any other Man, that ever existed?"[22]

Contemporary psychological continuity theorists, who see themselves as descendants of Locke, support their views with puzzle cases that are "higher tech" and more varied, but the basic strategies—and plots—are essentially the same. A typical argument is the "body-swap" case offered by Bernard Williams.[23] He asks us to imagine that persons A and B enter some sort of machine that switches the psychological life of A into B and vice-versa. We are to imagine, furthermore, that prior to this swap we

> announce that one of the two resultant persons, the A-body-person and the B-body-person, is going after the experiment to be given $100,000, while the other is going to be tortured. We then ask each A and B to choose which treatment should be dealt out to which of the persons who will emerge from the experiment, the choice to be made (if it can be) on selfish grounds.[24]

He argues that we are likely to find it most plausible and consistent for person A to choose that after the switch the B-body person be given the

[20]John Locke, *An Essay concerning Human Understanding*, ed. P. Nidditch (Oxford: Clarendon Press, 1979), p. 342.

[21]Ibid., p. 340, my emphasis.

[22]Ibid., p. 339, my emphasis.

[23]Bernard Williams, "The Self and the Future," in John Perry, ed., *Personal Identity* (Berkeley and Los Angeles: University of California Press, 1976). I should mention that in the end Williams questions the legitimacy of the intuitions evoked by this case, arguing that the same case differently described supports a bodily identity criterion. In the end, then, he does not himself support the psychological continuity theory. Nonetheless, he offers this case as a paradigmatic example of the sort of case that *is* used to support that view, and so my use of it is legitimate.

[24]Ibid., p. 181.

money and the A-body person the pain, and person B to choose exactly the opposite. What this shows is that we believe that after the operation person A will be in the body currently belonging to B and vice-versa. When psychologies switch bodies, then, we describe this event as one in which persons switch bodies rather than one in which they switch psychologies. There are a wide range of variations on such cases—many of which we encounter later—but in all of them psychological and physical continuity are separated, and it is assumed that we will concur that personal identity goes with the psychological life rather than the body.

If we look closely at these cases, we can see that they are driven by our intuitions about the four features. Consider, for instance, Locke's case of the prince and the cobbler. Locke tells us that we will all see that the cobbler-body is the same *person* as the prince, but that is because he is *accountable for the prince's actions*. The reason that the person with Nestor's soul cannot be construed to be the same person as Nestor is that he cannot be *concerned in his actions*. We are inclined to describe Williams's case as a body swap because we see that *self-interested concern* goes with the psychological life rather than with the body.

In each case our judgment of identity is based on judgments about its practical importance. We know that persons are responsible for only their own actions; we note that in the prince and cobbler case it seems appropriate to hold the cobbler responsible for what the erstwhile prince did, and so we conclude that he is the same person as the prince. We know we have a self-interested desire to be given $100,000 rather than be tortured, and so when we see which body in Williams's case we are inclined to have the money given to, we see who we think we are. Throughout the literature, we are asked to make our judgments about hypothetical cases by considering whether we think that the person described should "fear" what is going to happen to her, or be "nervous" about it or "relieved," or whether it should "matter" to her. These considerations about affect and practical results are not drawn as *consequences* of our judgments of identity when these cases are described, instead, they provide the basis for those judgments, and it is assumed that in each case the judgment will favor the psychological continuity theory.

It is not, of course, uncontroversially accepted that we must respond to these puzzle cases with these judgments, nor do *all* hypothetical cases support a psychological account of identity. It is at least fair to say, however, that the arguments for the claim that personal identity must be defined in psychological rather than bodily terms have proved extremely compelling, and this claim has enjoyed widespread acceptance. This view is not, furthermore, a creation of the philosopher's thought-experiment laboratory; it runs deep within our culture. The basic idea that what is important to us in personal identity is continuation of psychological life—regardless of the substance in which it is embedded—can be found in the numerous tales of metamorphosis and body transfer from ancient myths to the plots of television situation comedies. It can be found in William James's *Principles of Psychology* when he tells us that

> the Soul, however, when closely scrutinized, guarantees no immortality of a sort *we care for*. The enjoyment of the atom-like simplicity of their substance *in sœcula sœculorum* would not to most people seem a consummation devoutly to be wished. The substance must give rise to a stream of consciousness continuous with the present stream, in order to arouse our hope, but of this the mere persistence of the substance *per se* offers no guarantee.[25]

This intuition is also found in the widespread conviction that "surviving" an accident for twenty years in an irreversible vegetative state is no sort of survival at all, whereas a disembodied afterlife full of bliss (if such a thing were really to happen—we are not committed by this intuition to the claim that it does or could) would be a very nice thing, and certainly a way to survive.

I do not claim that these are the only intuitions we have about identity, nor do I deny that there are questions of identity that are best answered with a bodily criterion. I do, however, endorse the general Lockean claim that if our concern is with capturing our intuitions about the four features, sameness-of-substance views will not do. The puzzle cases that support psychological continuity theories are so puzzling, as Perry puts it, "because they seem to disprove the view that a person is just a live human body. . . . The abandonment of the simple theory that personal identity is just bodily identity carries with it the need to formulate an alternative account of personal identity."[26] In the past few decades a great deal of effort has been devoted to formulating such an alternative in the form of the psychological continuity theory.

The Psychological Continuity Theory

The basic form of the psychological continuity theory is obvious. Reidentification theorists want to tell us what makes a person-stage at t_2 and a person-stage at t_1 stages of the same person. Psychological continuity

---

[25]William James, *The Principles of Psychology*, vol. 1 (New York: Dover, 1950), p. 348.
[26]Perry, "Introduction," p. 5.

theorists believe that this relation is psychological continuity. They thus hold the view that a person-stage at t_2 is a stage of the same person as a person-stage at t_1 just in case the relation of psychological continuity holds between them (alternatively, we could say "if the person-stage at t_2 is psychologically continuous with the person-stage at t_1," or "if the stage at t_2 and the stage at t_1 are stages of the same psychological life").

This is a start, but obviously needs further development. The notions of psychological continuity over time and sameness of psychological life over time are no clearer, initially, than the notion of identity over time. The problem of specifying what is involved in the continuation of a single psychological life is similar in structure to any other question about the continued existence of a changing complex entity over time and is approached in the same way. The basic strategy, as we have seen, is to look at different temporal stages of the persisting entity and articulate what relationship must hold between them in order for them to be stages of the same entity. Here, then, we need to look at different temporal stages of a psychological life and ask what relation they must bear to one another to be part of the same life.[27] The relation in terms of which psychological continuity theorists specify this persistence is, roughly speaking, qualitative similarity.

Mere similarity is, of course, too crude a relation. No one would require that in order for a person's psychological life to continue for forty years he needs to have a psychological makeup in forty years that is qualitatively identical to the one he has now. Just as complex objects can change over time and yet still be said to persist, there is a general feeling that a psychological life, too, can continue in the way that is important to us even if it changes, as long as the change is gradual and lawlike.

The view I am describing is expressed in its basic contours by David Lewis, who tells us,

> I find that what I mostly want in wanting survival is that my mental life should
> flow on. My present experiences, thoughts, beliefs, desires, and traits of charac-
> ter should have appropriate future successors. My total present mental state
> should be but one momentary stage in a continuing succession of mental states.
> These successive states should be interconnected in two ways. First, by bonds of
> similarity. Change should be gradual rather than sudden, and (at least in some

[27]Richard Wollheim has a great deal of importance to say about the relationship between questions of personal identity, questions about the identity of the *life* of a person, and questions about what it is to lead the life of a person. See *The Thread of Life* (Cambridge: Harvard University Press, 1984), pp. 1–32. I have more to say about these connections and Wollheim's work in Chapter 5.

respects) there should not be too much change overall. Second, by bonds of lawful causal dependence.[28]

What is required to specify the notion of psychological continuity, then, is some account of just when change is gradual and lawlike *enough* to preserve continuity.

To offer such an account we need a way of quantifying similarity between person-stages, as well as some specification of the degree of similarity that is necessary to preserve continuity. Parfit offers an example (as far as I know the only *fully* articulated example) of such a specification. He begins the statement of his psychological criterion with some preliminary definitions. The first is of "direct connections," which are connections of the following sort: that between a memory and the experience of which it is a memory, that between an intention and the later act in which it is carried out, and the persistence of a belief, desire, or other psychological feature.[29] Parfit goes on to define a second relation: "psychological connectedness" that is, "the holding of particular direct psychological connections."[30] He then says that "we can claim that there is enough connectedness [for personal identity] if the number of connections over any day, is at least half the number of direct connections that hold over every day, in the lives of nearly every actual person. When there are enough direct connections, there is what I call strong connectedness."[31]

He thus takes, as the criterion of personal identity over time,

> The Psychological Criterion: (1) There is psychological continuity if and only if there are overlapping chains of strong connectedness. X today is one and the same person as Y at some past time if and only if (2) X is psychologically continuous with Y, (3) this continuity has the right kind of cause, and (4) there does not exist a different person who is psychologically continuous with Y. (5) Personal identity over time just consists in the holding of facts like (2) to (4).[32]

In basic form, Parfit's psychological criterion is a perfectly typical statement of the psychological continuity theory, but his version of this criterion differs from that of other theorists in some important respects, and it will be helpful to review these in order to get a more general picture of the psychological criterion.

[28]Lewis, "Survival and Identity," p. 17.
[29]Parfit, *Reasons and Persons*, p. 206.
[30]Ibid.
[31]Ibid.
[32]Ibid., p. 297.

Briefly, some of the important differences are these. First, Parfit's clause (5) takes a stand on the issue of reductionism that was discussed earlier. This clause commits Parfit to a reductionist view—a commitment that we have already seen is not universal. It also seems to commit him to a four-dimensionalist view of persons. If a person just *is* a collection of temporal stages of persons, then these stages must be genuine parts of the person, who cannot be wholly present at any time. This, too, is a controversial view. His clause (4)—the requirement that identity be "nonbranching"—is there to preempt a standard objection to the psychological continuity theory. (Parfit's clause [4] is one of several possible responses to this objection; the others and the objection itself are discussed in Chapter 2.)

Parfit's clause (3)—the requirement that psychological continuity have its appropriate cause—can be interpreted in a number of ways. Parfit's own view, which he calls the "widest" version of the psychological criterion, is the view that *any* cause is the right kind of cause—which is just to say that cause is not an issue for him. Others (such as Shoemaker) endorse what Parfit calls the "narrow" version of the psychological continuity theory. This view holds that in order to be identity-preserving psychological continuity must have its "normal" cause—where "normal cause" is generally cashed out in terms of the continued existence of the same functioning brain.[33]

This final difference deserves more consideration. It might seem that the the narrow and widest versions of the psychological criterion are quite separate views. As it turns out, the differences between them are inconsequential for our purposes, and where appropriate I show that this is so. The narrow version of the psychological criterion is, however, often thought to be an attractive means of reconciling the intuitions pulling us toward a bodily continuity theory with those pulling us toward a psychological continuity theory, and it is worth saying a few words here about why it is not, as this might defuse the inclination to turn to this version as a solution to difficulties with psychological continuity theories.

The impetus for the narrow version of the psychological criterion comes from the consideration of still more hypothetical cases. It is easy to imagine cases that seem to involve psychological continuity but not identity, and these appear to demand some sort of revision of the widest version of the psychological criterion. An example of such a case (albeit a controversial

---

[33] I should mention that Parfit describes a third alternative—the "wide" version, which holds that any *reliable* cause of identity is the appropriate cause. There does not seem much to motivate this view, and I think Parfit has a good argument against it (*Reasons and Persons*, p. 208). I do not, therefore, discuss it in detail here.

one) is Parfit's story of Teletransportation. Here we are to imagine some-one traveling to Mars by having blueprints made of all of his physical and psychological states; his original body is then incinerated, and a new individual built on Mars to the exact specifications of the blueprints. Although Parfit ultimately tries to use this case to support his psychological continuity theory, many view it as just the opposite. To many, Teletransportation is not transportation, but execution and replacement by a replica.

Interpreted in this second way this case seems to indicate that not every cause of psychological continuity is sufficient to constitute sameness of person. It shows that we can imagine cases in which psychological continuity is complete—perhaps even more complete than it usually is—and yet there is no personal survival. What is missing in these cases is precisely the continuation of the same physical entity. Thus it may be that without psychological continuity there is no continuity of person, but it seems that even with that continuity the same body must continue to exist if the same person is to continue to exist. This seems to indicate that sameness of body must be added to sameness of psychology for the continuation of the person.

Further investigation reveals, however, that the whole body need not persist for the person to persist—obviously a person can lose a finger or a limb, have a heart or liver transplant, receive an artificial knee, or get a haircut without loss of identity—it is only the brain (or at least a large portion of it) that seems *truly* necessary. The reasons for emphasis on this organ are obvious; to the best of our empirical knowledge it is the brain that produces our psychological lives. As Noonan points out, "the reason why . . . brain identity should be preferred to bodily identity as a criterion of personal identity is that it is the brain and not the rest of the body that carries with it psychological identity—identity of memory, personality and character."[34] We want to retain the brain because we believe that our memories and characteristics are stored and generated there. We assume, therefore, that transplantation of the brain would preserve psychological similarity, but loss of the brain would destroy it.

The intuitions drawing us toward a narrow version of the psychological continuity theory are powerful. I think, however, that they should be resisted, because by indulging them we gain plausibility at the cost of neglecting the original goal of analyzing our concept of personal identity. To see why this is so, we need to consider first what is doing the work in these cases.

[34]Noonan, *Personal Identity*, p. 9.

There are two reasons why we might respond as we do to puzzle cases like those supporting the narrow version of the psychological criterion. We might, as narrow-version theorists suggest, be discovering that sameness of brain is part of our *concept* of what is required for personal identity, but this seems unlikely. It is only because we have empirical reason to believe that it is the brain that causes the psychological continuity we value that we want to make it part of our definition of what constitutes identity. If we found that our assumptions about the brain's causal powers were mistaken, we would certainly no longer take it to be required for the continuation of the person. It is therefore not part of our *concept* of personal identity.

More plausibly, we might discover that not all psychological continuity is created equal. There is a certain *quality* of psychological continuity in our day-to-day lives, and it is *this* continuity which seems to be connected to the four features. We might feel that the continuation of the brain is necessary to our continued existence because it is only when we have psychological continuity produced in the ordinary way that we are sure we have *genuine* psychological continuity. In this case it would be the genuine continuity and not the brain itself that is conceptually necessary for identity. If we could be assured that we could have the same kind of continuity without the brain, then we would feel we had all that identity required without the brain, which is what the original Lockean intuitions suggest.

To get a better picture of what I mean here, consider a trio of cases. If I go to sleep and wake up as usual, it is obvious that this constitutes survival in our ordinary sense. If I am smothered in my sleep by a madman who has at the same time brainwashed my next-door neighbor to have exactly the states I would have had upon awakening had he not smothered me, it is pretty clear that this does not constitute survival in our ordinary sense. But if we imagine that I am smothered by the madman and then that someone wakes up on a cloud with wings and a harp just as I might have waken up at home had I not been smothered, the case is harder. Those who are unwilling to call this a case of survival generally feel this way because they do not believe that the scenario described is really possible, not because they feel that *if* it happened it would not constitute my continued existence.

What these cases are meant to demonstrate is that it is not the presence or absence of the brain itself that is really at issue, but the question of whether there is genuine psychological continuity or the mere appearance of such. In responding to them we presuppose that the continuity between my going-to-sleep self and my angelic self has a different *quality* than that between my going-to-sleep self and my brainwashed next-door neighbor.[35] Although the cases supporting the narrow version of the psychological criterion seem to contradict those supporting the view that psychological continuity is necessary and sufficient for identity, they do not. Instead they alert us that it matters to judgments of identity what *kind* of psychological continuity we have, and that the psychological relationship between person-stages described by psychological continuity theorists is not the continuity we care about—it is missing something. What needs to be added to the widest version of the psychological continuity theory to provide an analysis of our concept of identity is thus not the persistence of the brain (which presumably generates the deeper continuity), but a description of whatever qualitative features the psychological continuity ordinarily caused by the continued functioning of the brain has that the kind of continuity described by widest-version psychological continuity theorists does not.

To guarantee the right quality of continuity by stipulating that sameness of brain must cause that continuity is thus an unsatisfactory move within the context of an attempt to analyze our concept of identity. Sameness of functioning brain is, so far as we know, always coupled with the right kind of psychological continuity, and so it provides good *evidence* for the existence of that continuity. It is the continuity itself, however, that actually *constitutes* that identity, and a metaphysical criterion of identity owes us an analysis of the qualitative differences between the psychological continuity caused by the brain and that caused by Teletransportation.

Although I do not, for independent reasons, endorse Parfit's widest-version criterion, I do agree with him that if the kind of psychological continuity described in his criterion (excluding clause [4]) is qualitatively like ordinary psychological continuity, then it will not matter to us how it is caused. If, on the other hand, it is not qualitatively like the psychological continuity we value (which, I argue later, it is not), then simply adding the requirement of the persistence of the brain does not give us the kind of information we seek about the nature of the difference. Indeed, in such a case the criterion would be incoherent, since the kind of psychological

---

[35]Parfit will, of course, acknowledge that we feel this way, but deny that this feeling can have a basis. He tells us that it is not that Teletransportation is as good as ordinary survival, but that ordinary survival is as bad as Teletransportation, and what we want over and above the kinds of connections that the widest version of the psychological criterion provides simply cannot exist (*Reasons and Persons*, pp. 279–80). I speak to Parfit's arguments in later chapters—I know that I am not defeating them here, merely stating that I do not accept their conclusion. It is important to see, however, that I do not need to resolve this issue now. My immediate point is about what is driving our intuitions. Parfit is interested only in showing that these intuitions are without foundation—he acknowledges freely that they exist.

continuity caused by the brain would not be the kind described in the criterion.

There are, then, many different versions of the psychological continuity theory; they all, however, share two features. First, they start with the goal of offering a reidentification criterion for persons. Second, they accept the basic intuition that personal identity is constituted by psychological continuity. The goal of psychological continuity theorists is thus to provide a theory that defines the identity of persons over time in terms of psychological connections between person-stages at different times.

I contend that this project is incoherent. The goal of offering a reidentification criterion is fundamentally at odds with the goal of defining personal identity in terms of psychological continuity, because psychological continuity as we ordinarily conceive of it has a logical form much different from that of an identity relation. I contend that a psychological reidentification criterion can only stand by redefining the notion of psychological continuity until it is drastically different from our ordinary conception of that relation, and different in a way that is absolutely crucial. The notion of psychological continuity to which reidentification theorists are driven by the structure of their view does not seem to bear any relation to the practical importance of identity or to provide a plausible basis for survival, responsibility, self-interested concern, or compensation. By putting their intuitions into the form of a reidentification criterion, psychological continuity theorists thus undermine the original support for their view.

2

The Problems of Logical Form

The intuitive pull of the claim that personal identity must be defined in psychological terms is very strong. The attempt to articulate this intuition in the form of a psychological reidentification criterion, however, faces obvious and immediate difficulties. If a relation is to serve as a reidentification criterion, it must have the logical form of an identity relation. Psychological continuation, as we usually conceive of it, does not have this form, and so a variety of absurdities can be generated by using it as a criterion of identity.

A number of ingenious solutions have been proposed to remedy this problem. These allow psychological continuity theorists to avoid absurdity, but force them to redefine psychological continuation in a way that ultimately undermines their project. Our intuitions tell us, quite convincingly, that psychological continuation *as we ordinarily conceive of it* is the only relation that can underlie the four features (survival, moral responsibility, self-interested concern, and compensation). This relation cannot itself provide a logically consistent reidentification criterion, so psychological continuity theorists alter it until it can. What we find, however, is that when we consider the *altered* conception of psychological continuity our intuitions tell us just as strongly that *this* relation does not bear the importance of the four features.

In this Chapter I look in some detail at two of the most widely discussed objections based on logical form that have been raised against psychological continuity theories: the objection based on the intransitivity of psychological continuation and the objection based on the recognition that psychological continuation does not admit of degrees. I also describe two of the most successful responses to each objection. In the course of this discussion few concrete conclusions are drawn and a number of ends left loose. I should, therefore, explain here what I expect to accomplish.

First, I hope to show in a detailed discussion of the major replies to problems of logical form the gymnastics required to make the relation of psychological continuation fit the logical form of an identity relation. Second, I hope to point out a number of minor implausibilities that result from the moves psychological continuity theorists must make to avoid the problems of logical form. These are not sufficient in and of themselves to reject the view, but they are worth keeping track of—what recommends the psychological continuity theory is its intuitive appeal, and too many counterintuitive results may make us rethink our commitment to it. Third, and most important, I hope to show that satisfactory responses to the problems of logical form require psychological continuity theorists to adopt either a reductionist or four-dimensionalist view of persons.

In sum, the purpose of the discussion that follows is to show how a view we accept because of its commonsense appeal gets turned into a highly technical and alien philosophical theory, and in so doing, to set the stage for the more definitive arguments of Chapter 3.

The Transitivity Problem

A standard objection to psychological accounts of identity rests on the intransitivity of psychological continuation. It is obvious that if person A is the same person as person B, and person B is the same person as person C, then person A must be the same person as person C. It seems easy to imagine cases, however, in which person A is psychologically continuous with person B, and person B is psychologically continuous with person C, but person A is *not* psychologically continuous with person C. This raises serious problems for anyone defining sameness of person in terms of psychological continuity. Two major objections to psychological continuity theories in the literature are based on concerns about transitivity—the older of these comes from an objection raised by Thomas Reid against Locke; the more modern is linked to hypothetical cases of fission and duplication.

REID'S BRAVE OFFICER

Reid believes, like many others, that Locke holds a memory theory of personal identity—which means, roughly, that a person at one time is the same person as a person at another time if and only if the later person has a memory of one of the earlier person's experiences.[1] Reid objects to this view with his famous example of the brave officer. He asks us to

[1] I believe that Reid has misread Locke, but here I present Reid's objection in its own terms, because it obviously applies to contemporary psychological continuity theorists as well.

suppose a brave officer to have been flogged when a boy at school for robbing an orchard, to have taken a standard from the enemy in his first campaign, and to have been made a general in advanced life; suppose, also, which must be admitted to be possible, that, when he took the standard, he was conscious of his having been flogged at school, and that, when made a general, he was conscious of his taking the standard, but had absolutely lost the consciousness of his flogging.[2]

The problem, Reid argues, is that in this case Locke's view has the consequence that the general is the same person as the officer, and the officer the same person as the boy, but the general is not the same person as the boy, thus violating the transitivity of identity.[3] It is widely believed that Reid's objection is easy to circumvent. All that is needed is to change the relation required for identity from direct memory to the ancestral relation of memory and the problem goes away.

It is obvious that there is a parallel problem and solution with the broader psychological views of contemporary theorists. Psychological continuation is a relation that can fade—the general could be psychologically connected to the officer, and the officer to the boy, but the general not be psychologically connected to the boy. Similarly, the problem can be avoided by modern theorists if they define personal identity in terms of the ancestral relation of psychological continuation rather than continuation itself, and this is precisely what they do. Recall, for instance, Parfit's version of the psychological criterion. He starts with "strong connectedness"—which is composed of direct connections—but does not define identity in terms of this relation, but rather in terms of "psychological continuity"—overlapping chains of strong connectedness. Although strong connectedness is not itself transitive, the ancestral relation is, and so defining identity in terms of the latter rather than the former circumvents the transitivity objection.

This move is so efficient and universal that it is generally assumed that Reid's argument no longer presents any sort of difficulty for the psychological continuity theory. I am not convinced that this is so. Certainly a view that places identity in the ancestral relation of psychological connection rather than in direct connection does not have Reid's *transitivity* problem, but it is also not clear that it captures the relation we take to underlie the importance of personal identity. Locke's observation is, roughly speaking, that it is my direct conscious access to experience that makes it *mine*. This is

[2]Thomas Reid, "Of Mr. Locke's Account of Our Personal Identity," in J. Perry, ed., *Personal Identity* (Berkeley and Los Angeles: University of California Press, 1976), p. 114.
[3]Ibid., pp. 114–15.

not, however, the relation in terms of which psychological continuity theo-rists define identity. With Reid's objection in mind these theorists place identity in a weaker relation that does not demand direct conscious access to the actions and experiences that are ours—the ancestral relation of direct access. It is not obvious, however, that this weaker relation can rightfully claim to have all the intuitive appeal as the bearer of identity that the original relation had. In fact, psychological continuity theorists themselves make it clear that they attach much more importance to direct connections than to the weaker relation of continuity.

Parfit, for instance, tells us that although both psychological connected-ness and continuity are of some importance, "connectedness is more im-portant both in theory and practice."[4] Later, in discussing one of his many hypothetical cases, he imagines a world where there is "neither sexual repro-duction, nor division and fusion. There are a number of everlasting bodies, which gradually change in appearance. And direct and distinctive psycho-logical connections hold, as before, only over limited periods of time, such as five hundred years."[5] Although these people would be psychologically *continuous* with themselves, say, seven hundred years earlier, there would remain no *direct* psychological connections between the present person and the seven-hundred-year-younger person. In these circumstances, because of the lack of direct connections between temporally remote person-stages, Parfit argues that the pronoun "I" and facts about "identity" as defined by the psychological continuity theory would be basically useless for these people.[6]

Lewis considers a similar case and makes essentially the same point. He says:

> We sometimes say: in later life I will be a different person. For us short-lived creatures, such remarks are an extravagance. A philosophical study of personal identity can ignore them. For Methusaleh, however, the fading-out of personal identity looms large as a fact of life. It is incumbent on us to make it literally true that he will be a different person after one and one-half centuries or so.[7]

Lewis says further that for such persons "stages 200 or more years apart are R-related [psychologically connected] to such a low degree that what matters in survival is clearly absent."[8] Although overlapping chains of

---

[4]Parfit, *Reasons and Persons*, p. 206.
[5]Ibid., p. 303.
[6]Ibid., pp. 304–6.
[7]Lewis, "Survival and Identity," p. 30.
[8]Ibid., p. 33.

strong-connectedness may bear some importance, then, it is connectedness itself we intuitively take to carry the *primary* importance of identity.

The logical structure of identity requires that reidentification criteria define a transitive relation. Direct psychological connectedness, the relation that seems most closely linked to the importance of identity, is not transitive. The transitivity problem has been addressed by defining psychological continuity as the ancestral relation of direct connectedness, but this cure seems almost as bad as the disease. It does yield a transitive identity criterion, but this criterion lacks much of the appeal of the original, nontransitive relation.

I thus question the received wisdom that defining identity in terms of the ancestral relation of psychological connection completely answers Reid's Brave Officer objection. There is, however, another approach that can be taken to this kind of concern. It is developed in response to a more complicated transitivity objection raised in the modern literature.

FISSION AND DUPLICATION

A new twist is added to the old transitivity problem when we imagine the possibility of one person somehow splitting into two individuals, each of whom is psychologically continuous with the original. This kind of a split has been described in a number of ways—transplantation of brain parts, amoeba-like division, or an overzealous Teletransportation machine. Whatever the mechanism employed, these cases all describe situations in which each of two distinct persons, B and C, is psychologically continuous with some original person, A (fig. 1).

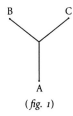

(*fig. 1*)

Although B and C are both defined as psychologically continuous with A, there is no reason to believe that after the split they will be psychologically continuous with each other. They will conduct their lives separately, move through different environments, have different experiences, and need not even know of each other's existence. This situation seems to commit the psychological continuity theorist to the claim that there can be a circumstance in which A is the same person as B, and A is the same person as C, but B is not the same person as C.

There are two basic strategies for answering this objection; one is exhibited in the responses offered by Parfit and Shoemaker; the other in those of Lewis and Perry.

The Parfit-Shoemaker Approach   Both Parfit and Shoemaker solve the transitivity problem by brute force. The problem here is that personal identity is defined in terms of psychological continuity, but psychological continuity is a relation that a person can bear to more than one individual. Parfit and Shoemaker both avoid this problem by modifying the definition of identity to say that it is constituted not simply by psychological continuity, but by *nonbranching* psychological continuity (recall Parfit's clause [4] in his definition of the psychological criterion). On this view, A at t_1 is the same person as B at t_2 iff A at t_1 is psychologically continuous with B at t_2 and *with no one else* at t_2. This means, however, that if A is psychologically continuous with both B and C at t_2, and B and C are distinct, then A is the same person as neither, since A bears the relation of nonbranching psychological continuity to neither.

This move does solve the transitivity problem, but it brings obvious and equally fundamental problems in its train. Shoemaker explains that the argument against his modified[9] psychological continuity view is not the transitivity objection because "we guarded the account against that objection by having it say, not that personal identity consists in psychological continuity *simpliciter,* but that it consists in *non-branching* psychological continuity. The objection is that this way of guarding against that absurd consequence makes the identity depend on something it cannot depend on."[10] The "something it cannot depend on" is, of course, the existence or nonexistence of another psychologically continuous subject.

It flies in the face of common sense to believe that A and B might be the same person if C does not exist, but not be the same person if C does; no facts about A and B are altered by the fact of C's existence. Most of us feel that the existence or nonexistence of some third person cannot influence whether A is the same person as B, because most of us believe that

[9]I call the Parfit-Shoemaker view a "modified" psychological continuity theory, even though in each case it is the original view offered by these theorists, because it represents a modification of our naive intuition that it is psychological continuity *simpliciter* that constitutes identity.

[10]Shoemaker, "A Materialist's Account," pp. 115–16.

whether a later individual y is identical with an earlier individual x can depend only on facts about x and y and the relationships between them: it cannot depend upon facts about any individuals other than x or y. Otherwise put, what the principle asserts is that whether x is identical with y can only depend upon the *intrinsic* relationship between them, it cannot be determined *extrinsically*.[11]

Call this the principle of intrinsic relation. There are, of course, some who reject this principle—not only Parfit and Shoemaker, but Nozick and other "closest continuer" theorists as well.[12] It is uncontroversial, however, that rejection of the principle of intrinsic relation is deeply counterintuitive, and it is important for us to be clear about exactly which intuitions it counters.

It is possible to generate a great many examples of just how strange it is to allow personal identity to be determined by features external to the relationship between the two people being identified. Let us consider some. According to Parfit's widest version of the psychological criterion, for instance, normal Teletransportation preserves identity. If I go to the Teletransporter and push the button and a replica appears on Mars, then on his view, the person on Mars is me. If, however, the overenthusiastic Teletransportation machine operator also beams my information elsewhere, and another replica is built, then there are two people psychologically continuous with me, and so neither of them *is* me—and I no longer exist. Even stranger, this is true whether anyone besides the second replica ever knows of her existence or not. According to this view, then, when my relatives come and pick me up at the Mars spaceport they should, by rights, be unsure whether their beloved niece has really made it to Mars, even as we sit in the car catching up on the family news.

Lest it seem that this worry is linked to some fact about the widest version of the psychological criterion, we should note that exactly the same concern can be generated (and in fact has been many times over) about the narrow version of this criterion. We can imagine the split here taking place as the result of the transplantation of the brain of one of a set of triplets into the bodies of her two sisters (one hemisphere into each, with the assumption that the hemispheres have identical function). In this case, the narrow version would say that either of the postoperative persons would be the same person as the brain donor if the other did not exist, but if both operations are a success, neither is the same as the brain donor, who thus no longer exists.

The strange implications of this view are familiar. It has been pointed out,

---

[11]Noonan, *Personal Identity*, p. 152.
[12]See Robert Nozick, *Philosophical Explanations* (Oxford: Clarendon Press, 1981).

for instance, that in such a circumstance the original donor would have a motive to bribe the hospital staff to make sure that an "accident" happened to one hemisphere of the brain before transplantation, thus ensuring her survival. Suppose the bribe is taken. Suppose A asks the surgeon to make sure that one of the hemispheres slated for transplantation is dropped on the floor, so that only B, but not C will awaken after the surgery. Imagine the remorseful surgeon finding himself unable to destroy a perfectly good half-brain, and secretly carrying on the second transplant anyway. When B awakens, with A's memories, she nervously asks the surgeon if he carried out "their little plan," the kindly surgeon reassures her that he did (crossing his fingers behind his back), and B is greatly relieved to find out that she, A, made it through the operation. We know, however, that C is hidden away somewhere in South America, and so poor B is mistaken, she did not really survive (at least not as A, which is who she thinks she is) after all.

Such cases are by now quite familiar. What I would like to emphasize here is what they tell us about the support for the principle of intrinsic relation. These cases not only show us that this principle has deep intuitive appeal, but that it appeals to exactly the same intuitions that provide the argument for the psychological continuity theory—intuitions concerning the four features. The cases described above sound absurd because in them the difference between identity and nonidentity, which is of tremendous significance, rests on something that does not seem as if it could carry that significance—the existence or nonexistence of another person.

Reconsider, for a moment, the brain transplant case. Our support for the principle of intrinsic relation is shored up by considering facts like the following. If I believe that I would survive if just my left brain were transplanted into another body, it makes no sense to believe I would fail to survive if this happened *and* another transplant (of my right brain) took place. If, in the transplant of just my left brain, I believe that the recipient would be responsible for my actions, it is hard to see how that person, who has not changed intrinsically, could be wiped clean of my misdeeds by the appearance of someone else. If I believe that my work will be compensated by rewards to the left brain recipient when there is only one transplant, it seems impossible that the existence of the right brain recipient in the double operation should nullify the compensatory effects of the left brain recipient's rewards. Finally, if I fear for the pain of the left brain recipient as I fear for my own, it seems grossly implausible that the existence of a right brain recipient could mitigate the pain felt by the left-brained person, and so there seems no good reason that knowledge of a second transplant should mitigate my fear.

My point in running through these well-known considerations is to show that our belief in the principle of intrinsic relation is tested in just the same way as our belief that personal identity must consist in psychological continuation and is adopted for just the same reasons. We believe that identity determines survival, moral responsibility, self-interested concern, and compensation; we also believe that only intrinsic features of the relation between persons at different times can affect these facts. We thus conclude that identity must be determined only by intrinsic features of the relation between persons at different times.

The primary argument for the psychological continuity theory is thus something like the following:

> A1: 1. Facts about personal identity are of great practical importance.
>   2. To account for the importance identity bears we must define it in terms of psychological continuation.
> ∴   3. Personal identity must be defined in terms of psychological continuation.

Whereas the primary argument for the principle of intrinsic relation is something like this:

> A2: 1. Facts about personal identity are of great practical importance.
>   2. To account for the importance identity bears we must accept the principle that only intrinsic features of two persons, and of the relation between them, can determine whether or not they are identical.
> ∴   3. Only intrinsic features of two persons and the relations between them can determine whether or not two persons are identical.

This presents a serious problem for theorists like Parfit and Shoemaker, who endorse a psychological continuity theory of identity that denies the principle of intrinsic relation. The support for the psychological continuity theory comes from its capacity to explain the importance of identity, but if it denies the principle of intrinsic relation it can no longer explain that importance. A psychological continuity theory that denies this principle is thus left with nothing to recommend it.

Both Shoemaker and Parfit respond to the anomalous implications of defining personal identity in terms of nonbranching psychological continuity, but neither response is satisfying. Shoemaker clears up some of the difficulties of this view by urging care about the referents of the terms we use in describing the fission case. Although this move avoids some objections, Shoemaker denies the principle of intrinsic relation and so fails to avoid the primary difficulty under consideration.[13]

Parfit, however, makes a more radical move that does speak directly to the objection we are discussing. The objection is that any philosopher who denies the principle of intrinsic relation seems committed to denying the relation between identity and the four features. Parfit resolves this difficulty by simply agreeing to do so. He expresses this view in his now-famous slogan, "Identity is not what matters in survival."[14] He acknowledges that our pre-philosophical intuitions tell us that in order for a person to survive there must be some person in the future who is he, but concludes that the fission case shows that pre-philosophical intuition to be misguided. His argument is simple. In the case where one person splits into two, there are only three possibilities. Either the original person is identical to *both* of the resultant persons; she is identical to one or the other; or she is identical to

---

[13]Shoemaker responds specifically to the worry that the nonbranching clause leads him to deny the necessity of identity. He seems forced to say that in the case where, for example, Brown's brain is split and only the left half transplanted into Brown, that Brown$_1$ is the same person as Brown, but might not have been if the right half of the brain had also been transplanted, creating Brown$_2$. Shoemaker denies that his view has this consequence. His point is that we need to be cautious with our use of terms, separating rigid from nonrigid designators. "Brown," "Brown$_1$," and "Brown$_2$" are rigid designators, but "the person with the left half of Brown's brain" and "the person with the right half of Brown's brain" are not. Since nonrigid designators are precisely those which can pick out different entities in different possible worlds, "the person with the left half of Brown's brain" might pick out a different person in the case where both halves of Brown's brain are transplanted than it does in the case where only one is. It is therefore no more problematic to say that the person with the left half of Brown's brain is the same person as Brown, but would not have been had the other half also been transplanted, than it is to say that the president of the United States in 1993 is married to Hillary but might not have been if Perot had won the election. What we are not entitled to say, however, is that Brown$_1$ is Brown, but might not have been. See Shoemaker, "A Materialist's Account," pp. 115–18.

This response seems to be an adequate response to the problem that the nonbranching clause violates the necessity of identity, but it does not address my concerns about the *importance* of identity. On this view, the person designated by "the person with the left half of Brown's brain" in the world where Brown splits and the person designated by that term in the world where only the left half of the brain is transplanted are different people, yet there is no difference whatsoever in the characteristics of these two persons and no reason why Brown should prefer the existence of one of them over the other. The difficulty with explaining the importance of identity that I have described is thus unchanged by Shoemaker's response. As Noonan points out, if we describe the fission case as Shoemaker suggests, then we "must acknowledge that in this case one could say to either of the fission products: 'You should consider yourself fortunate that the other fellow's brain transplant went so well—if it hadn't you would never have existed.'" Noonan, *Personal Identity*, p. 160.

[14]Parfit, *Reasons and Persons*, p. 217; see also pp. 262–63.

neither. We cannot choose the first option, because then the original person would be identical to two persons who were not identical to each other, and the transitivity of identity would be violated. The second option seems no better. Since the relation of the first person to each of the resulting persons is exactly the same, there are no grounds for claiming the person to be identical to one rather than the other. We must, therefore, choose the final option, which is what Parfit does.[15]

The case where a person splits, says Parfit, is a case where it seems clear that he survives—in fact, survives doubly—and yet we seem forced to the conclusion that there is no person in the future to whom he is identical. If this is true, then a person can survive into the future without there being anyone in the future who *is* she, which is to say that contrary to what we originally thought, facts about survival are *not* determined by facts about personal identity—identity is not necessary for survival. It should be clear that an exactly parallel case can be made for responsibility, self-interested concern, and compensation.

The claim that identity is not important in the ways we thought it was is deeply counterintuitive. It is, after all, the deeply held conviction that identity *is* important in these ways that supports the psychological continuity theory. Parfit recognizes this, but offers some considerations he believes make his claim more palatable. First of all, he has a story about why we believe identity is so important. Identity, he says, is a subspecies of psychological continuation—nonbranching psychological continuation. The importance that we *think* attaches to identity in fact attaches to psychological continuity, whether it branches or not. In our world, however, persons do not split into two, and so the only instances of psychological continuity we know are also cases of identity. It is easy for us, therefore, to misattribute the importance that attaches to psychological continuity to identity.

This story goes some way toward explaining Parfit's position, but it is still hard to accept. It certainly seems as if identity is *conceptually* rather than just empirically linked to survival, moral responsibility, compensation, and self-interested concern. It does not seem as if we simply observe that we hold persons responsible for their own actions and conclude (mistakenly as it turns out) that it must be the fact of identity that underlies our impulse to do so. Rather, it seems that we hold persons responsible for their actions *because* they are their actions, or feel they have survived *because* they are still around, and so on. Parfit realizes that even with his account of the origins of our mistake, we may still find his claim difficult to accept. He tries to clarify

[15]Parfit, *Reasons and Persons*, pp. 254–58.

his position still further by explaining that this result seems much less absurd if we adopt a reductionist view of persons.

Recall that for Parfit what it means to be a reductionist about persons is to hold that persons are constructs out of appropriately related person-stages. All that is required for a person at t_2 to be the same person as a person at t_1 on a reductionist psychological continuity theory is for the person at t_2 to be psychologically continuous with the person at t_1—nothing more is involved. One of the consequences of the reductionist view, Parfit claims, is that questions about persons can sometimes be empty—that is, we can lack no information and still be unable to give a confident answer to those questions. If fact F consists in nothing more or less than the holding of other, more basic facts, Parfit says, then in cases where some but not all of those more basic facts hold, we may, in a quite nonmysterious way, be unable to give a determinate answer to the question of whether or not F holds.

To clarify the idea of an empty question, Parfit uses the example of a club that meets then disbands, only to have several of its members reconvene some years later. He says that in this case the question "Is this the same club or a new one?" does not have a determinate answer. Since a club's being the club it is depends on more basic facts about members, activities, and so on, there is no fact of the matter about whether the club that meets after a hiatus is or is not the same club. The question of identity, Parfit says, is not the important question here. So long as we know all of the facts about who is meeting, where, when, and why, we know everything we need to. If we were not reductionists about clubs, but felt that there was some deep fact over and above facts about members and activities that determined club identity, then we would be right to be disturbed by our inability to give a determinate answer to the question of whether we have the same club. Since we are reductionists about clubs, however, this does not bother us.

Parfit suggests that we take the same attitude toward the identity of persons that we do toward the identity of clubs. The best description of the fission case, he believes, is as a case where the original person survives as both of the resulting persons, but is identical to neither. He points out, however, that there is no way to *test* what happens in this case. He says,

Suppose, for example, that I do survive as one of the resulting people. I would believe that I have survived. But I would know that the other resulting person falsely believes that he is me, and that he survived. Since I know this, I could not trust my own belief. . . . Even if we performed this operation, we would therefore learn nothing. Whatever happened to me, we could not discover what happened.

This suggests a more radical answer to our question. It suggests that the Reductionist View is true.[16]

If we are reductionists about persons, then when we know all the facts about psychological connectedness in the fission case, we know everything there is to know, and how we choose to describe the identities of the persons involved is unimportant.

Parfit's response to the transitivity problem, then, ultimately rests on a reductionist view of persons. We are at a loss to find an account of the identities of the persons involved in the fission case that seems completely happy, but we need not let that disturb us. All we need to know is that it is psychological continuity and not identity per se which is linked to the four features. If we believe this, it is not problematic that we are unable to come up with a determinate answer to questions about the identities of the persons in the fission case.

This response seems to avoid the immediate dangers of the transitivity objection, but is ultimately quite problematic in ways I describe in Chapter 3. For now, however, there are two observations that I wish to make about Parfit's response to the transitivity objection. First, we should note the extreme lengths to which he is forced in order to cope with the lack of fit between the logical form of psychological continuation and that of identity. Second, we should note that his response is very hard to accept without also adopting a reductionist view of persons. A psychological continuity theorist who wishes to take this approach is therefore pushed toward this philosophical commitment.

The Four-Dimensionalist Response (Lewis and Perry)   Lewis and Perry take an approach to problems of transitivity that relies on a view of persons as four-dimensional objects. From the perspective of the four-dimensionalist, the question of personal identity over time cannot be the question of what makes a *person* at t_2 the same person as a *person* at t_1, because there is no *person* at either t_1 or t_2. Persons do not exist *at* times, on this view, only *over* time. The question of personal identity must thus be the question of what relation a person time-slice at t_2 needs to bear to a person time-slice at t_1 if they are to be slices of the same person, and this relation will not be identity.

The *time-slices* that make up the life of some particular person are clearly *not* identical; instead they bear the relation of being parts of the same person. Perry calls this relation the "unity" relation and cautions,

---

[16]Parfit, *Reasons and Persons*, p. 258.

It is extremely important not to confuse the unity relation for an object with the relation of identity. Of course the two are connected in an important way. If a and b are . . . parts of an object of a certain kind K, and R_k is the . . . unity relation for Ks, then, if the K of which a is a part is identical to the K of which b is a part, a must have R_k to b. But, nevertheless, R_k is not the relation of identity, and must not be confused with it.[17]

Lewis calls the relation that all stages of the same person bear to one another the I-relation. He argues (as a psychological continuity theorist) that two person-stages are I-related if and only if they bear the relation of psychological continuity (which he, following Parfit, calls the R-relation) to each other. He then tells us that "it is pointless to compare the formal character of identity itself with the formal character of the relation R that matters in survival. Of course the R-relation among stages is not the same as identity either among stages or among continuants."[18] The claim that identity must be defined in terms of psychological continuity, on the four-dimensionalist view, is not the claim that if A is psychologically continuous with B then A is *identical* to B, but rather the claim that if two distinct person-stages, A and B, bear the relation of psychological continuity, then they are part of the same person. Psychological continuity does not play the role of an identity relation on this view, and so it is not surprising that it does not have the logical form of one.

More specifically, four-dimensionalists are able to respond to the transitivity objection as follows. Imagine the case where one person splits into two; A is a time-slice of the pre-fission person; and B and C are time-slices of post-fission persons (fig. 2).

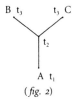

$(fig. 2)$

On the four-dimensionalist view this case is not to be described as one in which A is identical to B, and A is identical to C, but B is not identical to C. Rather, it is to be described as a case in which there are two continuant persons—one of whom includes A and B, and one of whom includes A and C. These two continuants are each, of course, self-identical, but they are distinct, and so there is no problem with transitivity.

[17]John Perry, "Can the Self Divide?" *The Journal of Philosophy* 69, no. 16 (September 7, 1972): 468.
[18]Lewis, "Survival and Identity," p. 21.

The four-dimensionalist's response avoids the transitivity problem, but it brings other problems in its wake. Most notably, there are anomalies involving the counting of persons at pre-fission times. Consider the case depicted in Figure 2. The four-dimensionalist's response to the transitivity problem involves claiming that this case depicts two distinct persons, both of whom exist between t_1 and t_3. This means, however, that there must be two persons located in the same body between t_1 and t_2. This consequence of the four-dimensionalist view, called the multiple occupancy thesis by Noonan, is at least initially quite disconcerting.

Lewis provides a very compelling statement of the difficulty we are likely to have with multiple occupancy when he says, "It is all very well to say from an eternal or postfission standpoint that two persons (with a common initial segment) are involved, but we also demand to say that on the day before the fission only *one* entered the duplication center; that his mother did not bear twins; that until he fissions he should only have one vote; and so on."[19]

Perry offers a similar statement of the problem. He tells us of the mishap of Jones who is split in the hospital into Smith-Jones and Brown-Jones and points out the difficulty for the four-dimensionalist view of answering the question "How many people were in Jones's room before the split?"[20] It seems, then, that this solution to the transitivity problem leads to a situation in which any of us could, as it turns out, be many of us, and this is difficult to accept.

Perry and Lewis endorse the multiple occupancy thesis and suggest ways to mitigate its implausibility. It is not important to go into too much detail about their views here, because the main point I am trying to make is simply that their response to the transitivity objection relies crucially on a four-dimensionalist view of persons. It is, however, worth saying a few words about their general strategy for dealing with multiple occupancy, which involves tensing statements about identity. Lewis suggests that although the continuant person containing A and B and the continuant person containing A and C are not identical *simpliciter*, they are identical *at all times* before the fission. They thus bear to one another a relation weaker than identity— the relation of tensed identity. Counting by identity *simpliciter*, says Lewis, there are two persons all along in Figure 2. Counting by identity-before-t_2 there is only one person, and counting by identity-after-t_2 there are two.[21] Perry's response involves adding a temporal reference not to statements of

[19]Lewis, "Survival and Identity," p. 26.
[20]Perry, "Can the Self Divide?" pp. 483–85.
[21]Lewis, "Survival and Identity," p. 27.

identity themselves, but to attributions of characteristics.[22] The two views are different, but in the same spirit, as Lewis puts it, "Perry and I have the same goals, but our priorities differ."[23] The multiple occupancy theory thus requires a major reconception of our ordinary sense of who populates our world, and with whom we are interacting. We take ourselves to be counting persons at times, and interacting with persons rather than person-parts; this view has the implication that we are, in these respects, mistaken.

It is also worth noting that there seems to be an easy way for the four-dimensionalist to answer the transitivity problem without endorsing the multiple occupancy thesis—although I have never seen anyone actually present this answer. It is one of the principles of the four-dimensionalist theory that *persons* do not exist at times, only parts of persons do. I do not see, therefore, why the four-dimensionalist cannot speak to the multiple occupancy problem by saying that in the situation depicted by Figure 2 there is no time at which it is correct to say that there are two persons present at t_1. Nor, for that matter, is it ever correct to say that there are two persons present at t_3. On this view it should always be incorrect to say that *any* number of persons exists at *any* time. All that can exist at a time are person-slices. In Figure 2, then, we have one person-slice at t_1 and two person-slices psychologically continuous with it at t_3; it is as simple as that.

Perhaps four-dimensionalists do not want to offer this response because they wish to avoid the conclusion that we cannot count persons at times. I do not, however, see how it can be avoided. If persons exist only over time, then it seems that what we are counting at any particular time must be person-slices and not persons. Consider the spatial analogy. If John, standing in the corridor, has put his foot over the threshold of the otherwise empty room next door, and someone asks me how many people are in that room, the correct answer is not "one" but "Well, John's got his foot in the door." I am not counting persons-at-places when I count spatial parts of persons, I am counting person-parts, and there is no reason why this should not hold in the case of temporal parts as well.

The four-dimensionalist may want to say that persons are *represented* at times by person-stages and so we can count persons at times by counting person-stages at times just as we can count persons in a room by counting heads. This analogy will not hold. What we are being asked to do is count persons at a *point* in time—a space of time into which no full-fledged person could fit. We might count persons in a *room* by counting heads, because the

[22]Perry, "Can the Self Divide?" pp. 484-85.
[23]Lewis, "Survival and Identity," p. 36.

persons are wholly present in the room and so their parts can represent them there. We would not, however, count persons at a *point in space* by counting *anything*. We do not expect to find *persons* in points of space, only spatial parts of persons. Analogously, if the four-dimensionalists are correct, we should not expect to find persons at points in time, only person-parts. Since the four-dimensionalist is committed to this claim anyway, it seems he might as well use it to answer the multiple occupancy problem. This response is, of course, no more intrinsically plausible than the multiple occupancy theory itself, but it helps to keep us clear on the commitments of the four-dimensionalist view.

The main purpose of this discussion has been to introduce the four-dimensionalist approach as one of the basic strategies employed in responding to the transitivity objection. What we have seen, then, is that the pressures of this objection lead psychological continuity theorists to either a reductionist or four-dimensionalist view of persons. In Chapter 3 I show that neither view is tenable. First, however, I should reinforce the conclusions of this section by considering a second problem of logical form that leads to the same consequences.

Determinacy and Degree

Another misfit between the structure of psychological continuation and the structure of identity is the ability of psychological continuity to admit of degrees, whereas identity must be all-or-nothing. Person A may be more or less like person B, but A either *is* the same person as B or *not*—there is no middle ground. Psychological connection on the other hand, can, as Parfit points out, "hold to any degree."[24] There are a variety of hypothetical cases offered to show this, but we do not even need to make up science fiction examples to demonstrate the possibility of degrees of psychological continuity; they are all around us.

The fading out of memory and other connections described in Reid's case of the brave officer happens to all of us. Most people are significantly less psychologically connected to themselves twenty years ago than to themselves five minutes ago. Furthermore, within intervals of the same duration there can be more or less continuity depending on one's stage of life and particular circumstances. There is likely to be a higher degree of discontinuity during childhood, or around certain transitional points in one's life, or in the face of anomalous situations (think of Golding's *Lord of the Flies*), than

---

[24]Parfit, *Reasons and Persons*, p. 206.

in calmer times. Even during quite ordinary stretches of psychological development, there are natural fluctuations in the stability of one's beliefs, values, desires, and so on.

It is more or less uncontroversial that the psychological connections Parfit and others describe can hold to different degrees. This raises a problem for psychological continuity theorists, however; if identity is to be defined in terms of psychological continuity, and continuity can hold to any degree, then it seems that the identity of a person at t_1 with a person at t_2 should be able to hold to any degree, and certainly it cannot. The responses to this problem once again split into two basic approaches, best represented by Parfit on the one hand, and Lewis on the other. Both the strategies employed to respond to this difficulty and my objections to them are very much like those described in the previous section.

PARFIT'S RESPONSE

Parfit responds to this problem as he did the transitivity objection—with brute force—and he faces similar difficulties with his response. To make identity all-or-nothing, Parfit takes the relation of psychological connectedness, which can hold to any degree, and uses it to define a new relationship, "strong connectedness," which cannot. He says there is strong connectedness when "the number of connections is *at least half* the number of direct connections that hold over every day, in the lives of nearly every actual person."[25] A person at t_2 either is strongly connected to a person at t_1 or is not—there is no middle ground here either. Parfit then defines personal identity in terms of overlapping chains of strong connectedness, and this relation admits of no degrees.

The problem, of course, is that this all-or-nothingness is achieved only by making an arbitrary decision that half the average number of connections that usually hold over every day in the lives of nearly every actual person is the number requisite to constitute identity from moment to moment. Once again it does not seem that the difference between identity and nonidentity—a difference of vast importance—can hang on one psychological connection more or less. Imagine, for example, that as I sit here typing, my present person-stage is connected to the previous one by *exactly* half the connections that hold every day in the lives of nearly every actual person. If there are overlapping chains of such connectedness going back to the person-stage who was here ten minutes ago (and it is nonbranching, and so on) then I am the same person who was here ten minutes ago. Now

[25]Ibid.

suppose that in the next moment, one connection is lost without a new one being added (say something as trivial as this: the car alarm that has been going off incessantly outside my window finally stops, and so I am no longer annoyed by it). On Parfit's view there is no longer strong connectedness between the present person-stage and the one a moment ago, and so the person who had been sitting here for the previous ten minutes is suddenly gone. Identity is made all-or-nothing on this view, but only at the cost of having to acknowledge that the abatement of an annoyance could be a death sentence.

Parfit is well aware that implications of this sort follow from his view of identity. He fully acknowledges that the line he draws to define identity is arbitrary and essentially without significance. He does not find this problematic for his view, however, for precisely the same reasons that he does not find the triviality of identity to be a problem in the transitivity case. He urges a reductionist view and suggests that from this perspective these apparent difficulties pose no problem, because from a reductionist point of view we can realize that what matters is psychological continuity and not identity itself.

What is different here, however, is that Parfit believes this problem of logical form can be used to provide an *argument* for reductionism. In discussing the transitivity objection, Parfit could only recommend the reductionist viewpoint as a means of making sense of his answer to that problem. By contrast, he claims that the ability of psychological connectedness to hold to any degree gives us independent reason to believe that the reductionist perspective is the right one. To see this, one must remember Parfit's explanation of how the difference between a reductionist and non-reductionist stance on persons can be cashed out in terms of the difference between believing that questions of personal identity must always have determinate answers and believing that they need not.

His argument involves imagining a hypothetical case containing a spectrum of operations, each of which changes the psychological makeup of the patient by just one feature more than the one before.[26] The first case in the spectrum involves a person being changed by just one psychological state— for example, one memory is erased and replaced by that of someone else (in the case Parfit describes, Napoleon). The second case involves two such

---

[26]Parfit actually considers three spectra—the psychological one I am describing, a physical spectrum, and one that involves both physical and psychological change. See *Reasons and Persons*, pp. 229-41. He does this to show that one must be a reductionist no matter what account of identity one chooses. Since our discussion takes place within the perspective of the psychological continuity theory, I discuss only the psychological spectrum.

changes, the third three, and so on. In the final case, the original person's brain is wiped clean and replaced with an exact duplicate of Napoleon's psychological life. If we believe identity to inhere in psychological connections, Parfit says, and if we believe that identity is always determinate (the nonreductionist position), this scenario is very problematic. It is clear that the first operation described is identity-preserving, and that the final operation is identity-destroying. If identity is always determinate, then there must be some case between the endpoints where the line is crossed, so that the operation on one side preserves identity, but the next operation does not. These two operations are distinguished from each other by only one psychological state, however, and so the difference between them is trivial. It seems entirely arbitrary to draw the line at some *one* case rather than just viewing all of the middle cases as borderline. Parfit thus suggests that the best choice is to accept the reductionist position.

He acknowledges, of course, that we *can* arbitrarily stipulate how much connection is needed for identity—he does so himself in his identity criterion—but this distinction does not carry much importance. He says, "By drawing our line, we have chosen to *give* an answer to this question. But, since our choice was arbitrary, it cannot justify any claim about what matters. If this is how we answered the question about my identity, we have made it true that, in this range of cases, personal identity is *not* what matters. And this is the most important claim in the Reductionist View."[27] According to Parfit, then, we can have determinate identity only if we are willing to acknowledge that identity does not matter much.

I have a great many difficulties with Parfit's spectrum argument independent of its reductionist conclusion. One of these is the overly atomistic view of our psychological life it presupposes. The argument only works (1) if there is no single value, belief, desire, character trait, or other psychological feature that is so central to a person's identity that its removal or alteration would be a catastrophic and not a trivial psychological change, and (2) if all of a person's psychological features are so independent of one another that any one of them can be changed without changing any of the others. Neither of these presuppositions seems plausible. It is in fact far more likely that the cases toward the middle of the spectrum would change the character of the psychological being we encountered so much that we would hesitate to call it a person at all—let alone more-or-less the *same* person.

The most important thing to realize here, however, is the reaffirmation of the strategy and commitments we saw in Parfit's response to the transitivity

[27]Parfit, *Reasons and Persons*, p. 240.

problem. Parfit makes psychological continuation conform to the logical structure of a reidentification criterion by adding arbitrary and ad hoc requirements. These make identity unimportant in and of itself, attributing the importance usually granted to identity to the more generic relation of psychological continuity instead. This does not trouble Parfit, rather it reinforces his earlier conclusions. Consideration of the problem of degree thus shows even more clearly how Parfit's solution to the problem of logical form commits him to reductionism.

LEWIS'S RESPONSE

It might seem that Lewis could respond to the problem of degree in more or less exactly the same way he responds to the transitivity objection. He could simply say, that is, that if one adopts a four-dimensionalist view of persons, one can see that psychological continuity is not an identity relation and so need not take the logical form of one. Things are not quite so simple, however. Even though psychological continuity is not supposed to be an identity relation on the four-dimensionalist view, it *is* supposed to be coextensive with the I-relation—the relation that holds between all and only time-slices that are slices of the same person. The problem arises because the I-relation, like identity, seems to be all-or-nothing; either two time-slices are time-slices of the same person or they are not. The objection based on problems of degree thus still applies to a four-dimensionalist psychological criterion.

Lewis, however, suggests a way around this objection. His response is somewhat complicated, but ultimately it allows him to define a sense in which the I-relation is a matter of degree and in all cases holds to exactly the same degree as the R-relation (psychological continuity). Lewis's argument begins with the claim that degrees of psychological continuity can be translated into degrees of personhood for the four-dimensional continuant person of whom they are parts. The idea is that the weaker the psychological connections between the person-stages that make up a person, the less of a person the aggregate is. He says that given the view that a continuant person is an aggregate of R-interrelated person-stages, "it is clear that personhood admits of degree to the extent that the R-relation does. We can say something like this: the degree of R-interrelatedness of an aggregate is the minimum degree of R-relatedness between any two stages in the aggregate."[28] A person is a *person* Lewis says, only to the degree to which it is R-interrelated.

[28]Lewis, "Survival and Identity," p. 34.

The mathematics of this strategy gets complicated when we realize that a person is not just an R-interrelated aggregate, but a *maximal* such aggregate. There may be a set of person-stages that are R-interrelated to quite a high degree but are part of a much larger aggregate that is R-interrelated to a lesser degree. In such a case, it is not clear whether we have a short-lived person who is a person to a high degree, or a long-lived person who is a person to a lesser degree. What Lewis says about this situation is quite curious. Considering a case where there is a short-lived aggregate R-interrelated to degree 0.9, which is part of a much larger aggregate R-interrelated to degree 0.88, he says that he is inclined to say of this aggregate that "it passes the R-interrelatedness test for personhood to degree 0.9, but at the same time it flunks the maximality test to degree 0.88. Therefore it is a person only to degree 0.02!"[29]

Lewis admits that this response is problematic, but before looking at the problem he cites, I wish to raise one of my own. I am perplexed about what exactly the "test for maximality" is, and how it can be passed or failed to a *degree*. Lewis tells us at the beginning of his paper that "something is a continuant person . . . if and only if it is an aggregate of person-stages, each of which is R-related to all of the rest (and to itself), *and it is a proper part of no other such aggregate*."[30] It would seem, therefore, that if something failed the maximality test at all it would be a person to degree zero—the definition makes it quite clear that an R-interrelated aggregate that is a proper subset of another such aggregate is not a person to any degree.

The ultimate difficulty is that with degrees of R-relatedness there is some ambiguity about what is and what is not an R-interrelated aggregate. It seems to me that assigning *degrees* of personhood based on the maximality of an aggregate is a very strange way to set things up. There is some appeal to the claim that the degree of psychological interconnectedness in the life of a person can influence the degree to which she is considered a person (indeed, this claim will be a central part of my view in Part II), but there seems no basis whatsoever to say that a segment of a person's life (say from age ten to age twenty) is itself a person, but to a lesser degree than the person from birth to death—this is just a misuse of words.

Lewis himself points out some other strange results to which the conflict between the demand to look for the highest degree of R-interrelation in defining identity and the demand to look for maximality of aggregate can lead. If we take the case of a Methuselah whose psychological life gradually fades out, for instance, no segment of that person will pass the test for

[29]Ibid.
[30]Ibid., p. 22, my emphasis.

personhood to any significant degree.[31] To avoid these difficulties, he asks us to suppose that R-relatedness can hold to any degree from zero to one and says that then "every number in the interval from 0 to 1 is a possible location for an arbitrary boundary between pairs of stages that are R-related and pairs that are not."[32] He calls this a delineation and points out that relative to a particular delineation, all of our questions are easily settled. Once the delineation is set, we can tell whether stages are R-interrelated, whether an aggregate of such stages is maximal, and hence whether a pair of stages is I-related. Furthermore, relative to any delineation the R-relation and I-relation coincide exactly, just as Lewis demands.

He next points out that we can also make these judgments relative to a *set* of delineations that are all in agreement. We can then say that the degree of relatedness is the size of the interval on which it holds. Lewis says, "suppose, for instance, that two stages count as I-related when we set the cut-off for R-relatedness anywhere from 0 to 0.9, but not when we set the cut-off more stringently between 0.9 and 1. Then . . . they are I-related to degree 0.9—the size of the delineation interval on which they are I-related."[33] This is a way of making I-relatedness admit of degree, and as Lewis concludes, "the degree of I-relatedness equals the degree of R-relatedness. In this way personal identity can be just as much a matter of degree as the mental continuity or connectedness that matters in survival."[34]

This response undoubtedly succeeds in making the I-relation and the R-relation coincide, but it seems to require some otherwise unmotivated moves to do so. I have already mentioned one—the sudden claim that a segment of a person's life is itself a person, but to a lesser degree than the more extended life. Another is one that Lewis himself points out. After giving the example described in the above paragraph, Lewis notes that though the stages described in this case are I-related to degree 0.9, "there may not be any continuant linking those stages that is a person to degree more than 0. It may be that any continuant that links those stages is both R-interrelated and maximal at only a single delineation."[35] This is a very strange consequence indeed. The I-relation is meant to be the relation that holds between stages that are stages of a single person. These stages are I-related to degree 0.9, yet they are not both part of any person who is a person to more than degree 0, which sounds like the claim that they are not

[31]Lewis, "Survival and Identity," p. 34.
[32]Ibid., p. 35.
[33]Ibid.
[34]Ibid., p. 36.
[35]Ibid., p. 35.

both part of any person at all. It is no longer clear, then, what it means to say they are I-related, except to say that they are R-related. This, of course, gives us a coincidence between the two relations, but not a very informative one.

Finally, note that Lewis's response to the problem of degrees seems to push him, too, toward a reductionist position. In the end he admits that personhood and personal identity are matters of degree, and that if we wish to give a determinate answer to the question of whether A is the same person as B, we can do so only by making an arbitrary decision. He says that his response to the problem of degrees of psychological continuity involves the idea that "when something is a matter of degree, we can introduce a cutoff point. However, the choice of this cutoff point is more or less arbitrary."[36] He acknowledges, then, that in order to be determinate and all-or-nothing, identity must be trivial and arbitrary, and this is just what Parfit points to as the hallmark of the reductionist position.

Lewis's response to the problem of degree thus contains a number of oddities. Most important, however, this response once again relies crucially on a four-dimensionalist view of persons (and suggests the need for a reductionist view as well). I argue shortly that these commitments present much more serious difficulties.

Our pre-philosophical intuitions tell us that it is psychological continuation that underlies the importance we attach to identity, and so it must be this continuation that constitutes identity. Our naive conception of psychological continuation does not, however, have the logical structure of an identity relation.

There are two primary strategies for correcting this situation. One is to make arbitrary decisions that allow us to redescribe psychological continuation so that it does have the logical form of identity, the other is to adopt a view of persons as four-dimensional objects. I have pointed to a number of minor problems with each of these approaches and shall go on to show deeper difficulties. It may seem that there is an obvious alternative response to these objections that I have overlooked. Perhaps the problems of logical form simply show that the psychological approach to defining personal identity is misguided and that a physical criterion would fare better; however, this response will not work either. First of all, we have established that our intuitions tell us that a psychological criterion is required to capture the four features. More important, however, Parfit, among others, has

---

[36]Ibid.

shown that a physical criterion is subject to the same difficulties of logical form.[37] Our best bet for a criterion of personal identity that captures that relation's importance is still a psychological criterion, but a theorist who wishes to offer such a criterion without logical absurdity is committed to either a reductionist or four-dimensionalist view of persons.

[37]See, for instance, Parfit, *Reasons and Persons*, pp. 234-36.

3

The Extreme Claim

We have seen that in order to provide a logically consistent criterion of reidentification psychological continuity theorists are forced to adopt either a reductionist or a four-dimensionalist view of persons. Yet these commitments undermine their original project by rendering them vulnerable to the objection that their views cannot account for the importance we attach to personal identity. This objection, which has been raised in a variety of forms since Locke first offered his account of identity, has been labeled "the extreme claim" by Parfit. It is not usually associated with either reductionism or four-dimensionalism, but is set forth as a general problem for psychological accounts of identity. It has, traditionally, been one of the most difficult objections for psychological continuity theorists to counter.

It is ironic (an irony that has gone largely unremarked) that the objection that has given identity theorists the most trouble attacks them at just the point that was supposed to be their greatest strength—the capacity to account for the practical importance of identity. This happens, I contend, because the form of the reidentification criterion forces these theorists to operate with a notion of psychological continuity quite different from our ordinary one. We generally assume that psychological continuity implies the continued existence of the same experiencing subject, and it is with this understanding that we assume that psychological continuity underlies personal identity. The demands of logical form, however, force a definition of psychological continuity that undermines this assumption and so deprives this view of its appeal.

I make the more specific case that because psychological continuity theorists must adopt either a four-dimensionalist or a reductionist view of persons to remain consistent, the psychological continuity theory cannot avoid the conclusions of the extreme claim, for there is no logically consistent version of this theory that can explain the relation of personal identity to the four features.

The Extreme Claim

The extreme claim, the objection that psychological continuity theories are unable to explain the importance we attach to identity, is not new. It was raised against Locke by Reid and Butler and is still widely discussed in the literature. The basic structure of this objection is quite simple; however, before describing it, I should point out that the extreme claim assumes that identity bears a certain practical importance, and it is only possible to give a clear exposition of the argument for this claim if we leave open the possibility that this importance might attach to identity itself. To provide an initial account of the extreme claim, then, I need to return to pre-Parfitian intuitions, putting to one side Parfit's assertion that identity is not what matters. Once I have shown how the extreme claim applies to any reductionist or four-dimensionalist psychological continuity theory, I can show that Parfit's assertion cannot mitigate its force.

I start, then, with the original argument for the extreme claim. The first premise of this argument holds that the four features require numerical identity—qualitative similarity will not do. Differently put, the first premise tells us that qualitative similarity of the psychological life of two distinct individuals, A and B, is not sufficient for A to survive as B, or for B to be held morally responsible for A's actions, or for A to have self-interested fear regarding B's pain, or for B to be compensated by rewards to A. The pull of this claim is easy to feel. Our pre-philosophical intuitions tell us that qualitative similarity is more or less irrelevant to self-interested concern, compensation, moral responsibility, and survival. Consider these statements in turn. Self-interested concern is an emotion that is appropriately felt only toward my own self and not toward someone like me. We all know the difference between fearing for our own pain and fearing for the pain of someone else. The difference here consists not in *degree*—I may care more about the pain of my beloved than about my own—but in kind. In my own case the fear is based on anticipation; I expect to *feel* the pain I am dreading. It may be the case that I care *more* about the future pain of a kindred spirit than about the pain of someone very alien, but I do not *anticipate* the pain of either. Psychological similarity without identity is thus not sufficient to engender self-interested concern.

Similarly, only benefits to *me* can compensate me for present sacrifices. Making Sally work after school so that she can go to college is one thing; making her twin sister work after school so that Sally can go to college is quite another. This is why people receive paychecks for *their* hours and not anyone else's. Again, similarity seems irrelevant here. It doesn't matter if the person who gets my paycheck is more *like* me than someone else; I am only compensated if *I* get the money. The same case can be made about moral responsibility. It is only fair to punish me for my actions, and not for the actions of anyone else, no matter how similar to me they are.

Finally, and perhaps most clearly, qualitative similarity does not seem enough for survival—the existence of a person in the future who has beliefs, values, desires, and so on very *like* mine does not seem to guarantee my survival any more than the existence of someone with a psychological life very different from mine does. Recall the example from Chapter 1: surely I would rather wake up tomorrow with partial amnesia than be smothered in my sleep by the evil genius who has also brainwashed my next-door neighbor to exhibit my psychological makeup. That my neighbor may believe herself to be me and acts as I would adds an eerie dimension to the whole ordeal, but it does not bring me any closer to surviving it. There seems, then, to be strong intuitive support for the first premise of the argument for the extreme claim: qualitative similarity is not a strong enough relation to underlie the four features.

The second premise of this argument is that the psychological continuity theory collapses the distinction between someone *being* me and someone being *like* me—that all identity amounts to on this view is psychological similarity between distinct individuals. This is so because psychological accounts of identity must define personal identity in terms of relations between temporal parts that are really distinct from one another. Locke's contemporaries emphasized the punctual nature of consciousness. Locke, as we have seen, holds that sameness of person is constituted by sameness of consciousness. Joseph Butler points out, quite reasonably, that it is not at all clear what the requirement that the same consciousness exist at two different times amounts to. He asserts that consciousness is "successive" and, therefore, "cannot be the same in any two moments, nor consequently the personality constituted by it,"[1] Reid lodges a similar complaint, arguing that "consciousness, and every kind of thought, are transient and momentary, and have no continued existence."[2] And even Locke acknowledges that "the same Consciousness" is not the same "individual Action" but "a present representation of a past Action."[3]

[1]Joseph Butler, "Of Personal Identity," in J. Perry, ed., *Personal Identity* (Berkeley and Los Angeles: University of California Press, 1976), p. 102.
[2]Reid, "Of Mr. Locke's Account," p. 116.
[3]Locke, *Essay concerning Human Understanding*, p. 337. I do not, as I mention later, believe that Locke ultimately holds that sameness of consciousness must be spelled out in terms of qualitative similarity between moments of consciousness, but he does seem to hold this picture of consciousness.

Saying that the same consciousness exists at two different times thus cannot be the same as claiming that *numerically* the same consciousness exists at both of those times. Reid and Butler therefore conclude that it can only mean that these two moments of consciousness are qualitatively similar. Reid says, for instance, that when Locke talks about sameness of consciousness at two different times, "these expressions are to me unintelligible, unless he means not the same individual consciousness, but a consciousness that is similar, or of the same kind."[4]

On Locke's view, Reid and Butler argue, there is no distinction between the *same* person existing at two times and two persons who are just *like* one another existing at those times, and so, they argue, this view cannot account for the importance identity bears. Butler, for instance, tells us that if Locke's view is correct,

> it is a fallacy upon ourselves, to charge our present selves with any thing we did, or to imagine our present selves interested in any thing which befell us yesterday, or that our present self will be interested in what will befall us to-morrow; since our present self is not, in reality, the same with the self of yesterday, but another like self or person coming in its room, and mistaken for it; to which another self will succeed tomorrow. This, I say, must follow; for if the self or person of today, and that of tomorrow, are not the same, but only like persons, the person of today is really no more interested in what will befall the person of tomorrow, than in what will befall any other person.[5]

Reid's criticism is quite similar. He, too, holds that the importance of identity requires a relation stronger than qualitative similarity, and that none is forthcoming from a theory that places personal identity in sameness of consciousness.

The conclusion of the extreme claim follows quickly from these two premises. If the relation of qualitative similarity between the psychological lives of distinct individuals is insufficient to underlie the four features, and if the psychological continuity theory provides a definition of identity according to which all it is for some future person to be me is for that person to have a psychological life qualitatively like mine, then the psychological continuity theory obviously fails to account for the importance of identity.

[4]Reid, "Of Mr. Locke's Account," p. 116.
[5]Butler, "Of Personal Identity," p. 102.

Modern Theories and the Extreme Claim

Although modern psychological continuity theories differ in many details from the view Reid and Butler criticize, an argument with essentially the same structure can be made against any version of the psychological criterion that holds either a reductionist or a four-dimensionalist view of persons. Before showing this I should note that the distinction between reductionist and four-dimensionalist views is, to a certain extent, artificial. It seems, first of all, that anyone who holds a reductionist view of persons must also hold a four-dimensionalist view. If a person is taken to be an abstract entity—a construct made up of person-stages—then continuant persons must exist *over* time rather than *at* a time, and person-stages must be parts of persons. Furthermore, there seem to be a number of factors— some of which we saw in Chapter 2—pushing a four-dimensionalist toward a reductionist viewpoint. There may thus be no real need to offer independent proofs for the assertion that reductionist theories are defeated by the extreme claim and for the assertion that four-dimensionalists are. For the sake of thoroughness, however, I show that the extreme claim applies to four-dimensionalist psychological continuity theories and then show that its application to reductionist views follows straightforwardly.

It is easy to make a prima facie case that the traditional argument for the extreme claim applies almost without revision to any four-dimensionalist psychological continuity theory. The first premise—that the relation of qualitative similarity between distinct individuals is not sufficient to underlie the four features—remains unchanged. What needs to be proved is that the second premise—that on the psychological continuity theory all it is for someone in the future to *be* me is for some distinct individual in the future to be *like* me—also applies. There is some sense in which this is an easy claim to make against four-dimensionalist psychological continuity theories. The defining characteristic of these criteria is precisely the view that the temporal parts of persons are real parts, distinct from one another. The four-dimensionalist response to the transitivity objection, for instance, rests precisely on the *distinction* between the unity-relation or I-relation for persons and identity. The person-stage at t_2 is not identical to the person-stage at t_1, and they are part of the same person only because they are R-interrelated; that is, related to one another by overlapping chains of psychological likeness. The four-dimensionalist thus does seem to provide a view in which the only relation there is between a person now and herself in the future is one of psychological similarity (worse yet, the weaker *ancestral* relation of psychological similarity) between distinct individuals. The second premise thus seems to apply to these versions as well, and the argument for the extreme claim defeats them.

Some examples bring this point home. If the four-dimensionalist psychological continuity theory is correct, it is hard to make sense of our practice of holding persons responsible for their own and only their own actions. The person-stage we put in prison for a murder cannot be identical to the person-stage who pulled the trigger on the gun. (As William Carter puts it, he "has a perfect temporal alibi, since [he] did not, strictly *exist* at the time of the robbery.")[6] The only relation between the agent who commits the crime and the time-slice who languishes in prison, on this view, is that they bear the ancestral relation of qualitative likeness, and it becomes difficult to see how punishing the present person for his past action is any fairer than punishing his twin.

Similarly, the person-stage slaving away now to rack up overtime is not identical to the person-stage who will soak up the sun in the tropics. The slaving person-stage cannot remain around long enough to enjoy the rum and warm breezes that are supposed to compensate her for the work, and the sunbathing person-stage will leave still another person-stage to pick up the tab. The four-dimensionalist's claim that the same person did the slaving and enjoying amounts to no more, in the end, than the claim that the time-slice who enjoys the vacation is *like* the time-slice who slaves, and we have already seen that this is not enough to provide compensation. Exactly parallel examples can be offered for self-interested concern and survival, and it would seem that the extreme claim applies easily to the four-dimensionalist's view.

Proponents of four-dimensionalism, however, are bound to object to this analysis. Person-stages are not identical to one another on this view, but *persons* are self-identical throughout their lives. Although the person-stage who goes to prison is not identical to the person-stage who pulled the trigger, the four-dimensionalist can say, the *person* who commits the murder and the *person* who goes to prison are one and the same. This is, in fact, precisely the response Noonan offers on the four-dimensionalist's behalf. He says,

> Commonsensically the proposition that the first prerequisite for moral and legal responsibility is identity through time is correct. But to endorse it, one does not need to deny that persons perdure [extend over time as opposed to enduring

6 William R. Carter, "Why Personal Identity Is Animal Identity," *LOGOS: Philosophic Issues in Christian Perspective* 11 (1990): 75.

through time]. For all this proposition says is that a man can only be punished for what *he himself*—not someone else—did. And the proponent of personal perduring can agree with *that*. It is just that, in his view, for a person to have done anything in the past there had to be a past stage of him which did the deed. But the past stage is not *someone else*.[7]

A four-dimensionalist, he thus argues, can accept the principle that identity is required for responsibility, compensation, self-interested concern, and survival, because this view does offer identity of *person* over time.

This response cannot, however, ultimately save the four-dimensionalist from the extreme claim. Instead, it points to the very conceptual difficulties that make this view so problematic—the question of just *who* is to be taken as the subject of experience. This is by no means obvious for the four-dimensionalist. In order to distinguish their view from the three-dimensionalist view of persons, these theorists need to acknowledge that person-stages are subjects of experience in their own right. It would make no sense to say that person-stages are to be given ontological status and then deny them subjecthood, and four-dimensionalists do not do so (you will recall in Chapter 1 where I quoted Lewis saying that a person-stage "talks and walks and thinks, it has beliefs and desires"). We can conclude, then, that on the four-dimensionalist view person-stages are subjects of experience (and agents of action).

Now, if person-stages are subjects, either they are the *only* subjects of experience or *persons*—that is, aggregates of person-stages—are also to be viewed as subjects. If person-stages are the only subjects, then the extreme claim obviously applies. The intuitions supporting the psychological continuity theory show that what we care about is the continuation of the experiencing subject. If justice is to be served, the same subject who chose to commit the crime must suffer the punishment, and the same subject who experiences the exhaustion of overtime should enjoy the warm breezes. I have self-interested concern for the future I expect to experience and feel I will not survive if I can anticipate no further experience at all. *These* are the intuitions that call for a psychological rather than a substance-based view of personal identity. We can *stipulate* that the person is anything we want it to be and so make it true by *fiat* that one and the same person had any two experiences we choose. What is needed to avoid the extreme claim, however, is a view on which *one and the same experiencing subject* can be present at two different times, and if person-stages are the *only* experiencing subjects for four-dimensionalists, they cannot offer such a view.

[7]Noonan, *Personal Identity*, p. 143.

These theorists thus need to claim (as Noonan's response implies) that there are *two* subjects, the person-stage *and* the person of whom it is part. But this move raises all kinds of questions about the relation between the experience of the two subjects. Presumably the experience of a continuant person at time t, and of the stage-at-t of that person, are identical in character—if the two could have different experiences at the same time the view would be untenable. But what does it mean to say that there are two subjects having the same experience in the same place at the same time?

The most defensible answer to this question is to say that the person-stage is the primary subject of experience and that the continuant person is its subject in only a derivative or abstract sense. This response would imply that it is the person-stage who *really* feels the experience, which is assigned to the person only as a sort of courtesy. On this view we can say of a person that he has any experience or takes any action that any one of his stages does, but must add that a person can only have an experience or take an action if one of her stages does it, as it were, *first*—where this indicates a conceptual rather than a temporal priority. Another way of putting this response is to say that all it *means* for a person to have an experience or take an action is for one of the numerically distinct person-stages that constitutes him to do so.

This response, however, leaves the four-dimensionalist once again vulnerable to the extreme claim. If the person-stage is the primary subject of experience, and if a person can experience only, as it were, *through* a person-stage, then it seems obvious that the units to which the importance of identity would attach would be the stages and not the persons. An example might help. Consider an offhand remark Lewis makes in discussing the question of what matters in identity. He says, "What matters is that one and the same continuant person should have stages both now and later. Identity among stages has nothing to do with it, since stages are momentary. Even if you survive, your present stage is not identical to any future stage. You know that your present stage will not survive the battle—that is not disconcerting—but will *you* survive?"[8] This is certainly an intuitively appealing description of what one cares about, but does it make sense on a four-dimensionalist's view? Within the three-dimensionalist perspective, it is obvious that what matters to me in survival is not that *this moment* of my life continue into the future. That is not only unnecessary to survival, it is an absurd and romantic wish; time marches on. Within the context of the four-

---

[8]Lewis, "Survival and Identity," p. 20.

dimensionalist view, however, the contemplation of tomorrow's battle takes on quite a different tone.

What I want to focus attention on is the referent of the pronouns in Lewis's question: "You know that your present stage will not survive the battle—that is not disconcerting—but will *you* survive?" The four-dimensionalist *must* insist on a distinction between the person-stage and the person, so I ask to which of these the pronoun "you" in the question refers. Who is worried about survival? And who is not disconcerted by the fact that the pre-battle person-stage will not survive? If the four-dimensionalist takes the option described above and holds that the person-stage is the primary subject of experience, then the "you" in Lewis's description of pre-battle reflection must apply to the person-stage who is doing the worrying, just as the referent of "I" in "I hope I survive the battle" must be the person-stage who utters it and not the continuant person of whom she is a part. The person-stage is the one who is present; the one who formulates the hope.

If person-stages are the primary subjects of experience, there is no good reason they should worry more about the continuant person than about themselves. The person-stage who knows it cannot survive the battle *should* be disconcerted. It might gain some sort of comfort from knowing that the person of whom it is a part will live on—just as a revolutionary might gain some comfort from knowing that "The Cause" will live on if he falls—but certainly the fact that this stage, a subject of experience in its own right, is about to fade out and experience no more, should be of grave and immediate concern to it if it sees things clearly. If person-stages are the primary experiencers, then those subjects forming hopes and fears and intentions *cannot* exist in the future toward which they are looking. They can correctly anticipate nothing, and so the extreme claim applies.

The only option left for the four-dimensionalist is to say that the *person* is the primary subject, and that person-stages are only secondary subjects. This is a perfectly reasonable position for a three-dimensionalist to take, but I do not see how a four-dimensionalist can endorse it. Person-stages on this view have psychological states; they take actions; they would themselves *be* persons if they were not part of a larger aggregate. How then is it possible that a perfectly good subject of experience suddenly takes on a different attitude simply because there are subjects psychologically like it nearby in time? I cannot imagine a good reason for saying that an aggregate of psychological subjects is somehow more *primary* than the individual subjects it contains, and I have never seen any argument for a position of this sort.

The dilemma for four-dimensionalists is thus the following. If we *really* see persons as the primary subjects of experience and hold that person-stages can only be said to have experience in a derivative sense, then it is hard to see how the four-dimensionalist view is really any different from the three-dimensionalist view—what content has been added by claiming that these stages are parts of *persons* rather than of their lives? If the four-dimensionalist view is to differ from the three-dimensionalist view (and it must if the transitivity objection is to be avoided), person-stages must be full-fledged experiencing subjects. If they are, however, then they, rather than the entire person, must be the relevant units for the four features. On the only understanding of the relation between persons and person-stages that makes sense then, the four-dimensionalist's view is vulnerable to the extreme claim.

It should be clear that this argument applies even more immediately to a reductionist position. The reductionist acknowledges quite happily that on her view the person is an abstract entity—a logical construct out of person-stages. An abstract entity, however, cannot itself experience anything except in the most metaphorical sense. If the person is *nothing more* than a set of person-stages, then certainly the person-stages are the primary subjects of experience. Since these stages are distinct from one another, the extreme claim can be leveled against any reductionist view.

Responses to the Extreme Claim

There have, of course, been many attempts to respond to the extreme claim, but none of these is satisfying in the end. Consider two elements of our previous discussion that I have so far ignored: first, the requirement by some psychological continuity theorists that identity-constituting psychological continuation be caused by the continued existence of the same brain, and second, Parfit's claim that identity is not what matters in and of itself. It may appear that one or both of these allow psychological continuity theorists to avoid the extreme claim. They do not, but it is important to see why.

It may seem that the narrow version of the psychological continuity theory, which places identity in psychological continuity caused by the continued functioning of the same brain, could avoid the extreme claim because it, unlike the widest version, provides a persisting entity that can be the subject of experience at different times. On this view, the brain that plans the crime languishes in prison, and the brain that suffers the overtime enjoys the vacation. It should be obvious with a few moment's reflection, however, that the brain does not provide us with the right kind of persisting subject to speak to our concerns here. We have already seen why in the discussion of the narrow-version psychological criterion in Chapter 1.

What the puzzle cases supporting the psychological criterion show is that continuity of brain can only contribute to the four features if it somehow brings with it the kind of psychological continuity that *can* underlie those features. What the extreme claim shows is that the *kind* of psychological continuation described by psychological continuity theorists—a similarity between distinct moments of consciousness—does not possess the quality we require.

Versions of the psychological continuity theory that require that continuity be caused by the continued functioning of the same brain merely give us a view in which we have a string of similar yet distinct experiencing subjects that are caused to be similar in a particular way. The experiencing subjects themselves, however, remain distinct, and so the extreme claim still applies. The Lockean intuitions show us that what we need for identity is the persistence of the conscious experiencing subject. Unless some argument is forthcoming that psychological continuity caused by the continuation of the brain has a different character from that caused in some other way, and unless we are given some account of the nature of this difference, the extreme claim must be taken to apply to versions of the psychological continuity theory that require the continuation of the same brain as well as to those that do not.

Parfit's assertion, that identity is not, in itself, important, has a more complicated relation to the extreme claim. There are two ways Parfit's assertion might seem to undercut the force of this objection. One is readily dismissed, but the other requires more discussion. Let me begin with the former. It may appear that Parfit can use his slogan that identity is not what matters in survival as a direct response to the extreme claim. This objection charges psychological continuity theorists with offering a view of identity on which that relation is unimportant. Since Parfit unabashedly asserts that identity is not as important as we thought it was, it may seem that the extreme claim is simply not a problem for him. This response to the extreme claim does not work.

To see why, we need to reconsider the context in which Parfit's assertion, that identity is not what matters, is evoked, and what it really amounts to. He makes this statement, we have seen, in response to the problems of logical form caused by the fission case. Parfit argues that in fission we have the elements of identity that support the four features without having identity itself, because it is the psychological continuity rather than the uniqueness that we really care about. He does not deny that identity—as a subspecies of psychological continuity—is a sufficiently strong relation to bear the importance we attach to it; he only argues that it is not *required* for that importance to be appropriate. The conclusion of the extreme claim, however, is that identity as defined by psychological continuity theorists is not *sufficient* to bear the importance we attach to it, and Parfit's "identity is not what matters" slogan carries no weight against that complaint.

There is, however, a way in which Parfit's claim that identity is not what matters can be used to raise a more serious challenge to the argument for the extreme claim. The first premise of this argument is that identity is necessary for survival, responsibility, self-interested concern, and compensation. This, however, is what Parfit explicitly denies, and so it may seem that he can reject the first premise of the argument, and hence its conclusion. This approach however, does not work either.

It should be noted, for one thing, that the first premise of the extreme claim could be rephrased so that it does not rely on any features of identity per se. Instead of saying that identity is necessary for survival, self-interested concern, compensation, and moral responsibility, all we need to say is that qualitative similarity between distinct individuals is *not* enough for the importance we attach to identity. This is, in fact, one of the ways in which I stated the premise at the outset, and there is certainly as much intuitive support for this phrasing as for the one involving identity. Starting with this statement, all we need do to complete the argument for the extreme claim is to show that the relation in which four-dimensionalists and reductionists place identity is no better than the relation of qualitative similarity in this respect, and this is easily done. The connection they offer—the ancestral relation of psychological continuity appropriately caused—is even weaker than exact similarity. If anything, because it is the ancestral relation that is required, the likeness is even more remote, and we have already seen that the requirement of cause adds nothing that helps against the extreme claim. The argument for this objection thus goes through with the revised first premise.

What is important to understand here is that even if Parfit could convince us that *identity* is not necessary for survival, moral responsibility, compensation, and self-interested concern, we would still believe that these require something more than the relation described by psychological continuity theorists. In discussing the extreme claim we have become a bit clearer on exactly what that something more is. The possibility of anticipation is absolutely key. In order to believe *I* will survive, I must believe that I can correctly anticipate future experiences; self-interested concern requires that I expect to feel the experiences about which I am concerned; compensation requires that I be able to reasonably expect to experience the compensatory rewards; and for moral responsibility to make sense, when I take an action I must expect that I will be the one who experiences its consequences.

Now, it may be, as Parfit insists, that I can bear this relation to more than one person—in cases of fission, for instance, I may be able to anticipate the experiences of two distinct persons in the future. If, however, the relation I bear to those two persons is the one described by four-dimensionalist or reductionist psychological continuity theorists, then I cannot reasonably anticipate the experiences of either. Instead of a double success (as Parfit describes it), we have a double failure. This argument thus shows not just that *identity* is unimportant on reductionist and four-dimensionalist psychological continuity theories, but that *psychological continuation itself* (as defined by these views) is unimportant.

Parfit's original argument, based on the fission case, takes the justification for the affect we feel concerning facts about identity to stem not from the identity relation itself, but from the relation of psychological continuity instead. What the argument of the extreme claim indicates, however, is that if reductionist or four-dimensionalist psychological continuity theories are correct, psychological continuity cannot justify these attitudes either. The result is that if such a view is accepted there is *no* justification for this affect—it is simply a mistake. This is a very radical and counterintuitive claim, and it applies to reductionist or four-dimensionalist views whether or not we accept Parfit's argument that *identity* is not what matters in survival.

Parfit is aware of this, and he, himself, does not suggest that his claim that identity is not what matters refutes the extreme claim. Instead, he acknowledges that his psychological criterion has the consequence that we are mistaken in some of our most fundamental beliefs and practices. He is willing to admit that a person's relation to himself in the past and future is no different in kind from his relation to others, and that there is no reason why we should attach the affect and importance we do to either identity or psychological continuity. Parfit's ingenious move is to refuse to see this consequence as a reductio of the psychological continuity theory, claiming it instead as an interesting result.

Parfit realizes that it strikes at the core of our most basic beliefs to say that our ordinary affect and practices concerning ourselves are unwarranted, but insists that this is what our investigation shows to be the case. He suggests that we accept and be educated by this anomalous result just as we are by other revolutionary findings. He even sees some immediate benefits to this discovery. For one thing, he says, it dissolves the conflict between self-interest and interest in others. On this view, one's reasons for treating one's future self well are not much different from one's reasons for treating others well—there is no deep difference between working for the benefit of one's own future self and working for the benefit of others. On this view the complicated conflicts between the demands of self-interest and of morality that often trouble us thus dissolve.[9]

Parfit suggests further that realizing how tenuous one's connection to one's future self is can make one worry less about future suffering. He says, "Suppose . . . that I must undergo some ordeal. Instead of saying, 'The person suffering will be me,' I should say, 'There will be suffering that will be related, in certain ways, to these present experiences.' . . . [T]he redescribed fact seems to me less bad."[10] Finally, he reports that recognizing how flimsy a thing survival is makes him feel better about dying. "Instead of saying, 'I shall be dead,'" he tells us, "I should say, 'There will be no future experiences that will be related, in certain ways, to these present experiences.' Because it reminds me what this fact involves, this redescription makes this fact less depressing."[11] Parfit, thus, simply refuses to see the inability of the psychological continuity theory to capture our fundamental pre-philosophical intuitions about persons as a *problem* with these views; he insists that it is our intuitions and not the psychological continuity theory which must be rejected in the end.

Although other psychological continuity theorists are less explicit in their rejection of our common conceptions than Parfit is, they implicitly employ the same strategy. Other responses to the extreme claim try to salvage some of our ordinary practices and attitudes concerning persons, but do so only by redefining them. Perry, for instance, argues that our primary concern is for our projects, and that we are especially concerned for our future selves because, being most psychologically like us, they are the ones most likely to carry them out,[12] and Jennifer Whiting argues that the general, second-order concern we have for ourselves is actually very much like the sort of concern we have for our friends.[13]

Although these approaches do provide us with reasons to care about our futures and our survival, it is obvious that they do not give us the kind of reasons we generally take ourselves to have. In particular, these views do not deny that the present person-stage, who is worrying about the future of the person, is a distinct experiencing subject from anybody existing in the fu-

[9]See Parfit, *Reasons and Persons*, chap. 14.

[10]Parfit, *Reasons and Persons*, p. 282.

[11]Ibid., p. 281.

[12]Perry, "The Importance of Being Identical," pp. 67–90.

[13]Jennifer Whiting, "Friends and Future Selves," *The Philosophical Review* 95, no. 4 (October 1986).

ture. What this means, however, is that the concern of the present subject for her future self can never be a concern based on anticipation. The current person-stage cannot expect to feel future pleasures and pains, and so the kind of concern it can appropriately have for a future segment of its life must be vastly different from the kind of concern we in fact do have. These responses thus acknowledge the fundamental assumption of the extreme claim—that there is no relation that legitimately bears the kind of importance we usually attribute to identity.

This approach is consistent, but we need to reflect carefully on why we should be willing to accept it. We started with the goal of offering an account of identity that would capture our intuitions about the connection of that relation to the four features. Psychological continuity theorists argue that we should accept their account of identity precisely because it is the only view that can capture those intuitions. Now, when we find that no logically consistent psychological criterion can capture these intuitions, psychological continuity theorists tell us that they must be rejected on the grounds that the psychological continuity theory cannot explain them. Surely it makes more sense to conclude that the psychological continuity theory has failed than to reject the phenomena we set out to explain.

Psychological continuity theorists might challenge this response in the following way. We are forced to reject our pre-philosophical intuitions, they might say, not just because the psychological continuity theory cannot account for them, but because it cannot *and* because the psychological continuity theory was always our best and only hope. The Lockean puzzle cases show us that if *any* theory of personal identity can make sense of our intuitions it is the psychological continuity theory. This theory has been so popular precisely because Locke offers such compelling arguments that the four features do not attach to the continuation of either body or soul, but only to the continuation of psychological life. Once a bit of reflection reveals what a weak relation psychological persistence really is, however, we see that even that cannot capture our ordinary intuitions about personal identity. The only view that seemed as if it might be able to support our practice of attaching a special and unique importance to that identity turns out to be unable to do so, and this forces the conclusion that that practice is insupportable.

This argument represents the strongest possible response to the extreme claim. If it really is true that no account of personal identity can make sense of the fact that identity matters to us in the way it does, then we must accept the conclusion that this fact cannot be made sense of. We have not yet, however, been shown that there is *no* account of identity that can capture these intuitions—only that there is no *reidentification criterion* that can, and this is quite another matter. In the introduction I observed that there is more than one way of asking (and answering) questions of personal identity. The analysis so far indicates that the form of the reidentification question and of the answer it demands prohibit an answer to that question which can capture the relation between identity and the four features. Parfit suggests that we reject our intuitions about survival, moral responsibility, self-interested concern, and compensation. I suggest that a happier and more plausible reaction is to give up the goal of explaining these intuitions with a reidentification criterion. I contend that a change of subject to the characterization question will provide a means of offering a different kind of identity theory, one that *can* capture the four features and so succeed where psychological continuity theories fail.

Conclusion

We have seen that it is not possible for a reidentification criterion to capture our intuitions about the link between personal identity and the four features, survival, moral responsibility, self-interested concern, and compensation. It is important to recognize that this discovery does not impugn the legitimacy of the reidentification question itself—only the expectation that an answer to this question should enlighten us about the four features. There are many contexts in which we have an interest in reidentifying a particular person—an adoptee searching for her birth mother wants to know whether the woman she finds is in fact the same person who gave birth to her; a researcher conducting drug efficacy studies wants to know whether the person being checked over now is the one to whom the drugs were administered; a bartender may wish to know if the person ordering a drink is really the twenty-one-year-old named on the identification card; an accident investigator needs to determine whether the person found at the crash site is the same as the person who bought the ticket.

There are pretty clear procedures for addressing questions of this sort. The type of evidence marshaled might include fingerprints, blood type, dental records, or DNA tests—all evidence that serves to reidentify a human body. This is no accident; when the reidentification question is considered on its own terms there is a strong intuition that it should be answered with a bodily criterion. Before going on I should say a bit to defend this claim and describe the role of the reidentification question in my analysis of personal identity.

As I explained in Chapter 1, it is a part of the landscape of work on personal identity that we have two sets of intuitions concerning persons: one pulls us toward the view that persons are to be identified with their bodies, and the other toward the view that they are to be identified with their psyches. The traditional response to this has been to place these two sets of intuitions head-to-head as competing answers to the same identity question—the question of reidentification. Psychological continuity theorists, emphasizing the strong practical importance of psychological features, argue that in the end the intuitions pulling us toward a psychological account of identity are more powerful than those pulling us toward a physiological one. Our impulse toward a bodily continuity theory derives, they argue, from the reliability of bodily continuation as a sign of the psychological continuation that really constitutes identity.

This argument has a great deal of initial plausibility, but as I have shown, its conclusion is not tenable. In order to be logically consistent, a psychological account of reidentification needs to distort our conception of psychological continuation to the point that the intuitions originally supporting a psychological account no longer apply, and so a psychologically based reidentification criterion cannot do the work for which it was devised. I offer an alternative understanding of the relation between the intuition that persons should be identified with their bodies and the intuition that they should be identified with their psyches. On my view these are not competing answers to a single question, but distinct answers to different questions. According to this approach, our inclination to identify persons with their bodies arises primarily within the context of the reidentification question and the inclination to identify them with their psyches arises primarily in response to questions of characterization.

Our concept of persons has a dual nature. On the one hand persons are objects in the world, whereas on the other they are subjects, with agency, autonomy, and inner lives. When we think of persons as objects, we are interested in reidentifying them and find ourselves pulled toward the view that persons are to be identified with their bodies. It is when we consider persons as subjects, however, that issues concerning personal survival, moral agency, self-interest, and compensation arise. In this context, I contend, we are mostly raising questions of characterization, not of reidentification, and so it is in conjunction with the characterization question that we find ourselves pulled toward the view that persons are to be identified with their psyches. The perceived tension between our competing intuitions concerning persons can thus be resolved by offering a physically based account of reidentification and a psychologically based account of characterization.

This approach leaves us, however, with a question about the relation between identity as determined by the characterization question and identity as determined by the reidentification question. It seems that these two need somehow to be brought together. For one thing, presumably questions of reidentification and of characterization can be asked about the same person. But if the reidentification question identifies the person with a body, and the characterization question with a psychological subject, how can these two fail to be in conflict? Moreover, in practice there seems to be a very close relation between questions of bodily reidentification and questions related to subjectivity. A bartender may be interested in determining whether the body before him is really the same as one born twenty-one years ago because he is worried about legalities. But the law that requires a person to be twenty-one years old in order to drink is based on the idea that under normal conditions there is a rough connection between the age of a body and the maturity of the subject associated with it. Similarly, we are concerned to determine whether the body currently in custody is the same as the one present at the crime because we think that fact is relevant to determining facts about moral responsibility.

In order to make our varied intuitions about personal identity cohere in the way I suggest, it is necessary to acknowledge that the reidentification and characterization questions are not completely independent and to show how they can be interconnected and yet provide very different perspectives on what identity entails. Roughly speaking, on the view I defend reidentifying persons via their bodies constrains (but does not determine) the kind of psychological configurations that can constitute a single psychological subject. On this view facts about the reidentification of bodies are indeed acknowledged to provide information crucial to settling issues about the four features and about identity in the sense at issue in the characterization question. Nonetheless, questions of characterization remain distinct from questions of reidentification.

On my analysis, then, the reidentification question survives the argument of Part I as a serious question of personal identity. My claim is that if this question is freed from the inappropriate demand that it capture the relation between personal identity and the four features, the arguments for a bodily reidentification criterion are overwhelming. Once we have clarified its legitimate province, then, pursuit of the reidentification question will most likely involve an investigation into the specific metaphysical problems with reidentifying human beings, as well as more generic metaphysical puzzles about reidentifying changing material objects over time.

I do not defend this claim in detail here, nor do I engage the reidentification question in what follows. My more immediate concern is with the characterization question, and with the attempt to understand the connection between personal identity and the four features. Survival, moral responsibility, self-interested concern, and compensation are linked to facts about characterization, not reidentification, and in Part II I develop a psychologically based account of characterization that illuminates the link between these features and identity. There are deep connections between human bodies and psychological subjects, as well as between issues of reidentification and of characterization. In order to appreciate these connections, however, we must first separate the various questions of identity and understand each strain of our concept of persons on its own.

Part II

Characterization

4

The Characterization Question

The goal contemporary reidentification theorists have set for themselves—providing a reidentification criterion for persons that captures the relation between identity and the four features—survival, moral responsibility, self-interested concern, and compensation—is incoherent and ultimately impossible to meet. This has led some reidentification theorists to conclude that the relation we assume in our daily commerce between identity and the four features is illusory. I have suggested that this conclusion is too hasty—no *reidentification criterion* can capture the four features, but that does not mean that there is no identity theory of any kind that can. The intuitive connection we make between identity and the four features can be vindicated and understood if we recognize that the question of personal identity is not monolithic, and that our intuitions linking identity to the four features arise not in the context of questions of reidentification, but rather in the context of questions of characterization.

The Characterization Question

It is necessary to begin with a clear understanding of the characterization question. Most simply put, this question asks which actions, experiences, beliefs, values, desires, character traits, and so on (hereafter abbreviated "characteristics") are to be attributed to a given person. Reidentification theorists ask what it means to say that a person at t_2 is the same person as a person at t_1; characterization theorists ask what it means to say that a particular characteristic is that of a given person. The most familiar examples of the characterization question are more specifically questions of which characteristics are *truly* those of some person (as opposed, say, to those which are his as a result of hypnosis, brainwashing, or some other form of coercion). Although the problem of determining which characteristics in a person's history are ones with which she can be *genuinely* identified may seem quite different from that of determining which characteristics are part of her history at all, I argue that these are not two distinct concerns, but points along the continuum of a single question—the characterization question. Before seeing how this is so, however, we should get a clearer sense of the general form of this question by looking at it in its most familiar guise—that of a question about a person's *true* identity. After using common instances of the characterization question to provide an initial sense of the question's form, I define the broader question, which is the one I ultimately consider.

It is useful to note first that the characterization question concerns the kind of identity that is at issue in an "identity crisis" and not the logical relation of identity that reidentification theorists try to define. The notion to which I appeal here is the general use of the term "identity" to refer to the set of characteristics each person has that make her the person she is.[1] In an identity crisis, a person is unsure about what those defining features are, and so is unsure of his identity. The characterization question seeks a means of resolving this kind of uncertainty and determining which characteristics constitute a person's identity.

This kind of identity question can be asked from either a first-person or third-person perspective, and we have virtually countless examples of each version from literature, philosophy, psychology, and everyday experience. There is, for example, Nora's famous revelation at the end of *A Doll's House*, where she awakens to the fact that the person she has presented (and believed) herself to be is a sham—a persona created by her father, her husband, and a restrictive society.[2] The play ends with the slam of a door as Nora leaves to discover what she truly believes, values, and desires; she leaves, that is, to discover who she really is. Similar questions are raised for Conrad's Marlowe in *Heart of Darkness* and Hawthorne's Young Goodman Brown. Each of these men discovers a core of evil in himself and in humankind, and so each is led to wonder about his own true identity as well as those of the "civilized" men and women who are his daily companions.

There is, however, no need to turn to fiction for examples of this kind of

[1]This is, of course, a very vague notion and needs considerable filling in. I have not said anything yet about how we determine these characteristics, or how we distinguish the characteristics that constitute identity from those which do not. We do not, however, need to understand all of the details of the characterization question yet. All I am trying to convey here is the very general idea that we have a sense of "identity" in which a person's identity is defined in terms of her characteristics, actions, and experiences.

[2]Although he uses the example of Nora in a different way, I am deeply indebted to Stanley Cavell—both in print (the introduction to *Pursuits of Happiness*) and in conversation—for impressing upon me the importance of Ibsen's play.

identity question; they can be easily drawn from news headlines as well. To start with a few extreme cases, there is a characterization question in the startled "Who are you?" we can imagine coming from Ted Bundy's fiancée when she discovers that the personable young law student with whom she meant to spend her life is a serial killer, or from the person who learns that his adored grandfather is a Nazi war criminal, or in asking whether Patty Hearst the heiress can be viewed as the author of the criminal actions of Tanya the revolutionary. There are, moreover, less extreme cases that bring up the same kinds of issues—for example, the question we may ask about whether the person we see so ruthlessly crushing her opponents in business is really the warm and loving wife and mother we know her to be at home, or the confusion felt by the person who finds that her husband, with whom she thought she had a storybook romance, has had a series of tawdry affairs.

Although such questions are not generally considered by theorists of personal identity, they have not been entirely neglected by philosophers. There are a number of sources in moral psychology and the theory of action in which a philosophical treatment of these kinds of questions can be found. Harry Frankfurt, Charles Taylor, Gary Watson, and others attempt to articulate what it is that makes a characteristic truly attributable to a particular person. Frankfurt offers a very clear statement of the problem in "Identification and Externality" when he says,

> We think it correct to attribute to a person, in the strict sense, only some of the events in the history of his body. The others—those with respect to which he is passive—have their moving principles outside him, and we do not identify him with these events. Certain events in the history of a person's mind, likewise, have their moving principles outside of him. He is passive with respect to them, and they are likewise not to be attributed to him. A person is no more to be identified with everything that goes on in his mind, in other words, than he is to be identified with everything that goes on in his body. Of course, every movement of a person's body is an event in his history; in this sense it is his movement, and no one else's. In this same sense, all the events in the history of a person's mind are his too. . . . But this is only a gross literal truth, which masks distinctions that are as valuable in the one case as they are in the other.[3]

His goal is to give a principle according to which we can make these valuable distinctions. The characterization question thus does not ask about "iden-

[3]Harry Frankfurt, "Identification and Externality," in A. Rorty, ed., *The Identities of Persons* (Berkeley and Los Angeles: University of California Press, 1976), pp. 242-43.

tity" understood as "the relation which every object bears to itself and to nothing else," but rather as "the set of characteristics that make a person who she is."

This shows the basic *form* of the characterization question, but more must be said to define the version of this question at issue here. In the examples given so far, the characterization question is concerned with discussing which characteristics are *truly* attributable to a person, as opposed to those which are his only in Frankfurt's "gross and literal" sense. This question is not itself broad enough to capture the four features. Certainly *some* importance attaches to the fact of whether a characteristic is attributable to a person in the most fundamental sense—often more than attaches to the fact of whether it is *truly* his (for example, a person cares more about whether a pain occurs in her history than about whether it is *truly* hers— whatever that would mean).

The four features attach to both kinds of facts—facts about which characteristics can be attributed to a person in the gross and literal sense, and facts about which characteristics are *truly* his. It may thus seem that on my view we need (at least) two identity theories to capture the four features—a theory of *literal* attribution and a theory of *true* attribution. This is, however, a misperception. On the view I defend, facts about whether a characteristic is attributable to a person in the gross and literal sense and facts about whether it is *truly* hers are not answers to different questions, but different answers to the same question.

On this view there is a single question—the question of whether a particular characteristic is attributable to a particular person—the answer to which admits of degrees. To see what this means, contrast this question with the question of reidentification. When we ask whether a person at t_2 is the same person as a person at t_1 the answer should be quite simply "yes" or "no." As we saw in Chapter 2, this causes no small difficulty for reidentification theorists. With many questions of characterization, however, the requirement of all-or-nothingness does not apply. If, for instance, we ask whether P_1 believes X or desires Y, the answer might be a simple "yes" or "no," but it might also be a longer story. We could be told "he believes X, but only half-heartedly" or "she says she wants Y, but she certainly doesn't seem to be very actively pursuing it" or "he believes X, but I bet if you pressed him he would be willing to give it up" or "her desire for Y is the driving force of her existence, it is what her whole life is about."

It is a familiar fact that a given characteristic can be attributed to a person to a greater or lesser extent—from merely appearing in his history to defining who he is. There are thus not two different questions—the question of what makes a characteristic part of a person's history and the question of what makes it truly hers—but rather one question with a variety of answers. This is as it should be—it is highly implausible to think of a person's *true* identity as something completely distinct from his *literal* identity, or even as some sort of an island within it. Instead, all of the characteristics that are part of a person's history are presumed to contribute to making up her identity. Some, however, play a more central role than others and are more truly expressive of who she is.

What this means is that to define a person's identity in the sense that is at issue in the characterization question, one must not only be able to know *which* characteristics are part of his history, but also their role in that history—one must know which of the included characteristics are central to who he is, and so part of his "true" identity, and which are incidental or misleading. The details of how one is to do this, as well as more evidence for the continuity between attributing a characteristic to someone in the literal sense and in the more robust sense, unfolds in later chapters. The discussion here is only meant to tap into common conceptions in order to provide a general idea of what I call the characterization question. This question asks which characteristics are part of the story of a person's life, and what role do they play in that story.

The characterization question as I have defined it is not, as I have already acknowledged, unrelated to the reidentification question. The question of whether action A is attributable to person P is obviously intimately connected to the question of whether P is the same person as the person who performed A. Indeed, the questions are so closely related that it may, at first, seem that they are really just variant forms of the same question. Asking whether a particular crime can be attributed to the person before us may, it is natural to suppose, be nothing more than asking whether the person before us is the same person as the person who committed the crime. I maintain, however, that although an answer to the reidentification question undoubtedly has implications for the characterization question—and vice-versa—the two questions are indeed distinct.

For now, I focus on one particularly salient means of distinguishing between these two questions—the logical forms of the questions themselves and of the answers they require. The reidentification question seeks to define a relation between *two distinct person-time-slices* that makes them slices of the same person. The characterization question, on the other hand, seeks to define a relation that holds between a *person* and *particular actions, experiences, or characteristics* that are hers. The relata in the answer to each question are thus quite different, and so the form of the relation itself will be different. This is a difference that makes a difference for our purposes.

The Viability of the Characterization Question

I suggest that a change of subject from the reidentification question to the characterization question is a fruitful approach to the goal of offering a view of identity that captures its relation to the four features. Before discussing the specific advantages that the characterization question has over the reidentification question in this regard, I note that a look at the original statement of our intuitions about the four features—the statement that was integral to the development of the psychological continuity theory—shows that there is just as much reason to read it as expressing intuitions about characterization as about reidentification. We are told, for instance, that a person can be held responsible only for *his own actions*, that there is a special kind of self-interested concern that a person feels only concerning *her own states*; that a person can be compensated for sacrifices only by *rewards that accrue to him*; and that if a person is to survive she must *have experiences* in the future. These claims are at least as easily understood as linking the four features to facts about characterization as to facts about reidentification, and so there is no reason to assume at the outset that it is a reidentification criterion rather than a theory of characterization that should capture our intuitions about them.

The reidentification question is not necessarily the right question to ask when we are concerned with the four features; there are many reasons to believe that the characterization question is the more appropriate venue in which to investigate the relation between these features and personal identity.

THE PROBLEMS OF LOGICAL FORM

It is necessary to realize first of all that the problems described in Chapter 2 arise not only because the form of a reidentification theory conflicts with the logical structure of psychological continuation, but because it conflicts with the logical structure of the relations that constitute the four features as well. In discussing the problems of logical form in Chapter 2 I emphasized how the standard thought experiments show psychological continuation to be intransitive, or a matter of degree. The cases also reveal, however, that these features are shared by the relations "survives as," "has self-interested concern about," "is morally responsible for," and "is compensated by." Indeed, because these thought experiments demonstrate circumstances in which each of these relations can violate demands of transitivity or all-or-nothingness, Parfit concluded that identity cannot be the relation that *matters*. What this shows, in a word, is that the relations comprising the four features—the relations psychological continuity theorists are trying to express in their theories—do not have the form of the criterion in which these theorists try to express them.

It is trivial to show, moreover, that an attempt to capture facts about the four features in a view with the form of an answer to the characterization question does not suffer from these same tensions concerning logical form. An answer to this question defines a relation that holds between a person and the actions, experiences, or characteristics that are his. This relation does not relate like terms, and so it is not even clear what it would *mean* to demand that it be transitive—it is not so much intransitive as nontransitive.[4] As to all-or-nothingness, we have already seen that facts about characterization admit of degree. Indeed, it is this ability to admit of degree that links the question of what makes an action part of a person's history at all to the question of what makes it truly hers.

These observations show that the goal of providing an account of characterization that can capture the importance of identity—unlike the goal of offering a reidentification theory that does—has at least the possibility of success. The misfit of logical form that ultimately undermines the project of reidentification theories does not apply to theories of characterization,[5] and this provides some initial measure of encouragement for the view that the four features attach to facts about characterization rather than to facts about reidentification.

The recognition that the relation of attribution defined by an answer to the characterization question can be a matter of degrees, and so has the capacity to express degrees of importance, points to an even stronger connection between facts about characterization and the four features. Not only do both attribution and the four features admit of degrees, but degrees of these features seem to correspond to and depend upon degrees of attribu-

---

[4]It is not so much that the relation of attribution defined by the characterization question is *intransitive* as it is that the notion of transitivity does not apply to it. Suppose A is the action of P, then to even set up a question of transitivity there would need to be some B that is the action of A, and we would then need to ask whether B was also the action of P. But actions are not attributable to actions, and so the second step does not even make sense.

[5]As I have already acknowledged, this does not yet rule out the possibility that the characterization question might fall prey to other, equally serious, problems. I believe it does not, and I do speak to this issue in Chapter 5. For the time being, however, it will be quite instructive to see how this theory avoids the problems that undermine the project of reidentification theorists.

tion. Seeing how each of the four features can be a matter of degree, and how those degrees relate to degrees of attribution, can thus be helpful in demonstrating the kinds of connections that can be drawn between the four features and the characterization question.

Before going through the details of this discussion, however, I need to clarify what I expect it to accomplish. My major goal in this chapter is to loosen the grip of the assumption that the four features must be captured by a view with the form of a reidentification criterion. I hope, therefore, to show that it is at least as plausible to understand our original intuition (that facts about identity underlie the four features) as saying that facts about characterization play this role as it is to understand our original intuition according to the standard interpretation—that facts about reidentification do. To this end, I am trying to uncover intuitive links between the form of the characterization question and the form of the relations that constitute the four features. In the next several sections I describe how degrees of the four features are taken to correspond to degrees of attribution. But here— and this is important—I intend not to argue for the existence of links between attribution, and survival, responsibility, compensation, and self-interested concern, but rather to describe certain common pre-philosophical intuitions about these links. Because my goal here is only to understand better the intuitions that provide the impetus for the psychological continuity theory, I ignore some of the questions and challenges that have been raised to these intuitions. More conclusive evidence that the links we see intuitively do in fact exist is introduced in later chapters.

Degrees of Moral Responsibility   Consider moral responsibility. There is, of course, a great deal of controversy about exactly what an attribution of moral responsibility involves and requires, but there is broad consensus that facts about the centrality of an action to a person's identity (in the characterization question's sense of "identity") are highly relevant to moral judgments. It is a commonplace that a person can be more or less responsible for a given action that occurs in his history—a person is less responsible for tripping on a rock and knocking someone down inadvertently than he is for willfully pushing someone out of the way, and less responsible for willfully pushing someone out of the way when he is under duress, or there is some compelling reason to do so, than in ordinary circumstances. A person is not held as responsible for what she says or does when hypnotized, brainwashed, or under incredible stress as for what she says or does with a clear head, free from any form of coercion.

Whether we actually want to say that a person is not responsible for what he does when under duress, or that he is responsible but the duress is a mitigating factor, the fact remains that the degree to which an action expresses someone's identity is a central consideration in making moral judgments about it. The degree to which an action expresses a person's identity is, moreover, precisely what the characterization question seeks to determine. An account of characterization should tell us whether a particular action is something that merely occurs in a person's history (seemingly a minimum requirement for any kind of responsibility), something that is quite solidly hers, or something that flows naturally from features absolutely central to her character. And it is just this kind of information we use when we determine that the hired killer is more culpable than the woman who kills to protect her infant or the person who kills accidentally when his car has a blowout and he loses control. These kinds of considerations are reflected in our laws and in our ordinary practice and show a clear link between facts about moral responsibility and facts about characterization.

Degrees of Self-Interested Concern   A similar case can be made for self-interested concern. There is a basic sense in which one cares about each and every experience that occurs in one's history—all things being equal, pleasure is preferable to pain. (It is this level of concern on which reidentification theorists have focused.) The desire to feel pleasure rather than pain is an important part of self-interest; however, it seems unnecessarily restrictive to view this as the totality of the interest persons feel in their own lives. There is obviously a great deal more.

Persons are interested in the pursuit of their desires, the nurturing of their interests, and the furthering of their personal growth and development. They are interested in expressing their values and making their mark on the world. This can be summarized by considering self-interested concern as the concern a person has with being in a position to fulfill her desires and pursue her goals. This broader definition includes the already-noted concern persons have with pleasure and pain, since almost every person has a powerful (if not always compelling) desire to feel pleasure rather than pain. An interest in fulfilling one's desires and pursuing one's goals thus automatically includes a concern with pleasure and pain, but it includes more as well. It includes, for example, a concern with personal development, self-expression, making a difference, or doing something significant.

It is important to recognize these broader interests because they play a fundamental role in determining the appropriate limits of a person's self-interested concern and also show important links between this concern and the characterization question. To see this it is essential to remember first the widely recognized fact that a person's immediate desires are to be distinguished from his considered desires. A person has a prima facie interest in the fulfillment of every desire he experiences—the satisfaction of desires is pleasurable and their frustration painful. Simply pursuing desires as they occur is, however, a notoriously bad strategy for living a satisfying life. Desires conflict with one another by their demands on time and resources. If a person does not consider which desires are most worthy of fulfillment, it is all too likely that she will end up satisfying minor and insignificant desires at the expense of significant ones.

Self-interested concern can be thought of as the interest a person has in being in a position to pursue her *considered* desires under conditions of full information. The question, then, is what determines what these are—what considerations are applied to determine where a person's interests really lie? There are, of course, a number of factors that go into such a judgment. One is the sheer amount of pleasure and pain that that desire's fulfillment or frustration will cause. A person may forgo the pleasure of smoking to avoid the far greater pain of lung disease. There are, however, other scales on which desires are measured and compared, and other kinds of importance that can be attached to the fulfillment of desires besides their capacity to bring about pain or pleasure.

A person may, for instance, continue smoking *despite* knowing that he is likely to suffer greatly by doing so, because he has a considered commitment to the life of a bon vivant, to living fast and dying young, to staring mortality in the face and laughing. Here it is not, strictly speaking, a greater pleasure that makes the predicted pain worthwhile, but the ability to do what one believes to be most important with one's life. It is a commonplace that a person will find it in her interest to sacrifice a great deal more for goals or desires she takes to represent something important than for those she believes to be trivial. (Indeed, how much a person is willing to sacrifice for a goal is usually a measure of how important she takes it to be.)[6]

It is possible to generate countless examples of this phenomenon. We are all familiar with the sacrifices people are willing to make for their religious convictions, their art, their relationships, their political causes, their principles, or even things others might consider frivolous (for example, their wish to meet a particular movie star or own a particular object). If a person takes his work as an attorney to be fundamentally important to his life, he will undoubtedly forgo the satisfaction of a great many other desires in the

---

[6] I say "usually" because it is possible for a person to be mistaken about what is genuinely important to her, and so be willing to make great sacrifices for something that is not really very important to her all things considered.

interest of furthering his career. If he views the company softball games as nothing more than a moderately pleasant way to spend a few Sunday afternoons, on the other hand, he is unlikely to make too many serious sacrifices to play in them. Similarly, a woman who has dedicated herself to raising her children will obviously need to give up the satisfaction of a great many other desires in order to do so. She may well decide, on reflection, that it is worth it to her to make those sacrifices, because it will allow her to pursue the goal she takes to be most important. At the same time, however, she may be unwilling to make the same level of sacrifice to keep her car bright and shiny, or to buy an outrageously expensive floor-length evening gown (although there are some people who might make major sacrifices to fulfill these goals). It seems wrong to describe this simply by saying that she wants to raise children *more* than she wants to have a clean car or an elegant gown, or that she has sacrificed her own interests for larger goals—it seems rather that she thinks the former goals are more important and worthwhile than the latter, and so she has more of an interest, all things considered, in pursuing them.

What is significant for our purposes is that the question of which desires and goals a person takes to be important enough to sacrifice for is precisely the question of which desires, goals, and values are most internal to him. Recall the smoker who is willing to sacrifice his health. He does so to live the life that he believes he should be living. He is, he believes, a bon vivant, and to cave in to the pressures of body or society would be to live falsely—to be coerced by external pressures. Consider further the other two cases described above—the attorney and the mother—it is common in such cases to talk about a person's identity being completely bound up in his career or her children. The idea that the goals and values of central importance to us define who we *truly* are is fairly common, and so facts about degrees of identity play a central role in determining a person's true self-interest.

This connection has not, of course, gone unnoticed in philosophical discussions of moral psychology. To name just two contemporary examples, it is emphasized by both Taylor and Frankfurt. Taylor distinguishes between "simple weighers" and "strong evaluators," saying,

> The simple weigher's reflection is structured by a number of *de facto* desires, whereas the strong evaluator ascribes a value to those desires. He characterizes his motivation at greater depth. . . . Whereas for the simple weigher what is at stake is the desirability of different consummations, those defined by his *de facto* desires, for the strong evaluator reflection also examines the different possible modes of life or modes of being of the agent. Motivations or desires don't only

count in virtue of the attraction of the consummations but also in virtue of the kind of life and kind of subject that these desires properly belong to.[7]

Persons, he says, are strong evaluators, and their determinations of which desires to pursue are made in accordance with this deeper kind of evaluation.

Frankfurt famously distinguishes between first-order and second-order desires. First-order desires are the "de facto" desires described by Taylor, the ones that simply occur in our history. Second-order desires are desires about desires; they concern which first-order desires we want to have. A person may, for example, have a strong second-order desire to have first-order desires to nurture her family and may deplore particular first-order desires that compete with or undermine these. Frankfurt argues that those first-order desires which are endorsed by second-order desires are more truly one's own than those which are not and points out that in our considered judgment it is worth repudiating and frustrating even very powerful first-order desires that are not so endorsed.[8] Frankfurt seems to indicate that our true interests are determined by those desires and goals which have second-order endorsement. Once again, then, facts about the *degree* to which particular states are attributable to a person are seen as crucial to determining that person's overall interests.

How facts about characterization are related to self-interested concern is perhaps most easily seen by looking at cases where a person's identity is confused or in question. Cases like Ibsen's Nora show vividly that it is possible for a person to be mistaken about her identity, and hence about her interests. Prior to her revelation at the end of the play, Nora believes that her role as a particular kind of wife and mother is centrally important to her. She has, therefore, cheerfully made major sacrifices to fulfill that role. What she discovers in the end, however, is that she was mistaken. The goals and desires she thought were important to her are not—they are instead important to her husband, father, and the society in which she lives. She thus concludes that the sacrifices she made were not worth it—not because of some surprising fact about their yield, but because the principles for which they were made are not ones in which she truly believes.[9]

---

[7]Charles Taylor, "Responsibility for the Self," in Gary Watson, ed., *Free Will* (Oxford: Oxford University Press, 1983), p. 117.

[8]See, for instance, Harry Frankfurt, "Freedom of the Will and the Concept of a Person," in Gary Watson, ed., *Free Will* (Oxford: Oxford University Press, 1983), pp. 81–95.

[9]Obviously there can be many ways in which a sacrifice turns out not to have been worthwhile, and some of these have nothing to do with identity. Sometimes the world just does not comply with our plans and we do not achieve what we had hoped to, and sometimes things fall

It turns out, then, that Nora has not, despite what she thinks, been acting in her true interest, or placing her self-interested concern where it most appropriately lies. Such situations are quite familiar. It is easy to imagine someone realizing, for example, after an intense love affair has ended that the political cause on which he had worked so tirelessly, and to which he had devoted so much of his time and energy, is not nearly so important to him as he had thought. The desire to change the world in this way was not *his* desire, but that of his ex-beloved which he mistakenly took to be his own. Now, with a clear head, he sees that although he may have been willing to sacrifice a great deal for the *relationship*, he was mistaken in believing that it was worth it for him to sacrifice as much as he did for the *cause*.

A more extreme example can be found by imagining someone deprogrammed from cult membership, looking at her sudden poverty, her severed relationships with her family, her lost career opportunities and friends. Such a person might conclude that she has been unwittingly making sacrifices for the wrong values, values that were not truly hers, but were imposed upon her. The state of identity crisis in which a person like this finds herself after such an awakening is the state of being unsure of what she finds most important, or what is worth making sacrifices for.

Self-interested concern thus connects to the characterization question in the following way. First of all there is a certain primitive concern we have for the character of any state that will be ours at all—we care whether it will be pleasurable or painful. Furthermore, we have a special concern for our desires and goals and the beliefs they express. The goals and desires that occur in a person's history are not, however, all equally his, and so a person should not be equally concerned with the fulfillment of every desire or goal that occurs in his history. For a person to have *self-interested* concern for the fulfillment of a desire, that desire must, to be sure, at least be part of his history. Among those goals which fulfill this minimal requirement, however, the degree to which any particular goal is attributable to a person is at least part of what determines the degree to which he should be concerned about it, and so facts about characterization play a significant part in determining the limits of self-interested concern.

---

our way and so a sacrifice turns out to have been unnecessary. In Nora's case and cases like it, however, the situation is different. Her sacrifices turn out not to be worth it even though the yield is exactly what she expected—it is a reevaluation of her goals rather than a surprise about what is required to achieve them that leads to her conclusion. (Admittedly in this case the reevaluation is prompted by an unexpected revelation about her husband, but this is only the occasion, not the content, of her change.) In later chapters I say a great deal more about what is involved in this sort of judgment.

Degrees of Compensation   After a discussion of degrees of self-interested concern, the discussion of degrees of compensation follows easily. This is because facts about compensation are conceptually linked to facts about self-interested concern. To see this, all we need to do is recast facts about compensation in terms of desires and goals as we did facts about self-interested concern. Instead of emphasizing the compensation of present pain with future pleasure, as reidentification theorists do, we can broaden our definition by saying that a person is compensated for forgoing some desires by being put in a better position to fulfill others—for example, a student can be compensated for giving up her desire to play by the fact that studying hard now will get her the grades she needs to get into medical school, thereby giving her the opportunity to fulfill her lifelong dream.

The connection to issues of self-interested concern is obvious. The question of compensation, perhaps even more than the question of self-interested concern, revolves around what is worth sacrificing for what. The degree to which a given individual is compensated by something obviously depends (at least in part) on how internal the goal it allows him to fulfill— a sports-hating opera lover could not be compensated with season's tickets to the Bears games in the same way that an avid football fan could; and although admission to medical school might be compensation enough for major sacrifices to someone who desperately wants to be a physician, it is not going to be adequate compensation to someone trying to be a physician in a half-hearted attempt to please her parents.

Of course, for person P to be compensated by reward R the receipt of that reward must at least occur in that person's history, and this is what reidentification theorists emphasize—attempting to provide a means of determining whether the person who receives the reward is the same person as the person who made the sacrifice. What the above reflections show, however, is that the situation is subtler than that. Those rewards which accrue to a person in the fundamental sense of being part of his history can be more or less his and compensate him more or less accordingly.

Degrees of Survival   Finally, there are questions of survival. It may be hardest of all to believe that survival admits of degrees or that it is linked to issues of identity in the sense of characterization rather than reidentification. A brief review of the considerations initially raised in support of the psychological continuity theory, however, lends credence to these claims. To begin it is important to acknowledge that there are many different notions of survival that play important roles in our lives. There are, for instance, strictly biological conceptions of survival[10]—at some level we say that so long as the human organism we associate with a particular person is still living the person has survived, and that when the organism dies the person is no more.

Although this is a very central sense of survival, it is not the one that is of most interest for our present purposes. The thought experiments appealed to by psychological continuity theorists reveal another notion of survival that seems even more important to us—psychological survival. Indeed, the Lockean puzzle cases indicate that much of the importance we attach to biological survival is parasitic on the more fundamental importance of psychological survival. These cases suggest that we value biological survival mostly because we believe that it is probably required for psychological continuation. We have seen, furthermore, that biological survival without psychological continuation does not constitute the sort of survival we care most about, whereas the continuation of psychological life without physical survival does. It seems, therefore, that psychological survival is the kind of survival that is most important to us and is, at any rate, of great significance. It is this kind of survival which I propose to show admits of degrees and is linked to facts about characterization.

To see how there can be degrees of psychological survival, we should look at a continuum of cases. First, consider a case of irretrievable loss of conscious experience. Few would deny that this constitutes a very literal sort of psychological death. There are, however, less extreme cases that involve continuation of consciousness of a deficient sort. Contemplate, for instance, the late stages of Alzheimer's or some other form of vicious and irreversible dementia. To imagine this happening is to imagine one's self—the self one wishes to continue—ebbing away. Although this is not as complete an example of psychological demise as irreversible coma, it does not seem entirely hyperbolic to consider it a type of personal death.

From here, however, we can move on to even less extreme examples. Consider, for instance, someone who has long been the victim of a violent, abusive spouse. Such an experience can lead to marked personality changes. The battered spouse may become timid, fearful, and intensely focused on survival and on avoiding the wrath of the abuser. She may sever the relationships that had been central in her life; suppress her own desires, reactions, and characteristics; and concentrate on doing and being what her abuser requires. Such a person might have trouble identifying with the bouncy

[10]It should be noted, furthermore, that even when we are thinking only about *physical* survival, there are several different definitions of that concept as well.

teenager she sees in a high school photo, even though she knows that she is the human being depicted. She may find it impossible to remember how it felt when life seemed full of promise, or that she wanted to be a journalist, or what kind of house she wanted to live in—she may no longer be able to find her true desires, but only those her abuser wishes her to have. Similar effects can be found in other types of traumatic existence—addicts, members of personality-destroying cults, prisoners of war, and hostages are likely to suffer in similar ways.

We often describe such people as having "lost their identities," say that they "are no longer the same person," that "the person we knew is gone," and so on. My suggestion is that these statements need not be considered entirely metaphorical. It would be foolish to insist, of course, that losing one's identity to an addiction or abusive spouse is *the same as* losing it through irreversible coma or dementia—obviously it is not. Irreversible loss of consciousness is clearly much more like nonexistence than addiction is. I do want to claim, however, that these two conditions are points on a continuum. That what the addict, prisoner of war, or abused spouse is being robbed of is, in a very real sense, his or her *life*.

It may be tempting to argue here that I am confusing quality of life with life itself. Those who lose their identities in the sense described above may have less pleasant lives than those who are self-actualized, this objection would contest, but they are just as much alive. This is not, however, entirely obvious. There is a clear sense in which it is reasonable to say that those living under such extreme duress and coercion that their lives are in no way self-expressive are indeed less alive than a person in ordinary circumstances—just as the person with Alzheimer's who is fully conscious but suffering dementia is less alive than the same person acting as a fully functioning adult twenty years earlier.

This notion has wide currency. In his popular book *Listening to Prozac* Peter Kramer describes how Prozac changed one patient, whom he calls Sally, from a timid, retiring, social misfit to an outgoing, vivacious, and sociable woman. He expresses concern that the medication may have changed her personality too much, saying: "I felt concern that Sally may have 'overshot,' that this new personality was too different from her old one. She demurred. She said the Prozac had let her personality emerge at last—*she had not been alive before taking an antidepressant*."[11] We can make perfect sense of this utterance, and it seems unwarranted to insist that it be taken as a *mere* metaphor. Although the patient making the claim clearly

[11]Peter D. Kramer, *Listening to Prozac: A Psychiatrist Explores Antidepressant Drugs and the Remaking of the Self* (New York: Viking, 1993), pp. 147-48; my emphasis.

was alive even while depressed, she is, in a very real sense, *more* alive later on.[12] Aliveness, it seems, can have degrees, and if aliveness can have degrees, then so can survival—a person survives to only a limited degree if his degree of aliveness is diminished. Furthermore, the degree to which a person is alive, and hence survives, seems linked to the degree to which her actions, experiences, and characteristics are her own—the degree to which her identity is expressed in her life. Degrees of survival are thus linked to degrees of identity in the sense that is at issue in the characterization question.

The foregoing discussion shows one way in which the form of the relation the characterization question seeks to define is more congenial to expressing facts about the four features than the reidentification question is—the four features, like characterization (but not reidentification), can be a matter of degree. Reidentification theorists can, of course, account for degrees of identity, and hence for degrees of the four features. We have already seen how they do this in Chapter 2. We have also seen, however, that it is not natural to the form of a reidentification criterion to admit of degrees, and in order to make theirs do so psychological continuity theorists need to bend our notions of both psychological continuation and identity in ways that make them vulnerable to the extreme claim. Since the form of the characterization question is *naturally* suited to accounting for degrees of identity, the characterization theorist has no such problem.

Indeed, we have seen more generally that the form of the characterization question is in harmony with our intuitions about the four features, and that an attempt to capture these intuitions in a theory of characterization does not run into the difficulties of logical form that are so problematic for reidentification theorists. Such an attempt does not run into the related problems raised by the extreme claim either.

THE EXTREME CLAIM

In some sense the rest of this book constitutes my argument that the characterization question is not subject to the extreme claim. What I wish to do here, however, is provide some preliminary grounds for believing this by showing that unlike the form of the reidentification question the form of the

---

[12]In Chapter 6 I have a great deal more to say in defense of the claim that our talk about degrees of survival and aliveness should be taken literally. For now, however, it is enough to see that there is a clear sense we can give to the claim that survival can be a matter of degree, and that these degrees are linked to the kinds of information provided by answers to the characterization question.

characterization question does not make an account of characterization *automatically* subject to the objection posed by the extreme claim.

In Chapters 2 and 3 I emphasized how the attempts to avoid the problems of logical form make reidentification theorists subject to the extreme claim. We can arrive at the same conclusion from a somewhat different angle if we think about how temporally distant actions are attributed to a present person via a reidentification criterion. If, for instance, we wish to know whether the person we are about to punish robbed the bank, the reidentification theorist can only tackle this question by reading the question, "Did this person rob the bank?" as the question, "Is the person we plan to punish the same person as the person who committed the crime?" This may seem a very natural reading, but it has important—and not very natural—consequences.

The phrasing that is forced on reidentification theorists draws a wedge between the criminal and the recipient of the punishment which is not easily bridged. It requires that we first attribute the crime to one person (or person time-slice) and then attribute the punishment to an independently definable person (or person time-slice) and then ask whether these two persons are the same (or whether these two person time-slices are slices of the same person). The problem is that this means we can only attribute the crime to the person receiving the punishment *indirectly*—it must first be attributed to a past subject and then attributed to the present subject only via its connection with the past one. The need to define these two subjects independently, which reidentification theorists must do to avoid circularity, makes it impossible to attribute the past crime directly to the presently existing subject. We have already seen, however, that if the crime is not attributed directly to that subject we cannot define a strong enough relation between the subject to whom it is attributed and the subject we plan to punish to make the punishment justifiable (the same argument holds, of course, for self-interested concern, compensation, and survival).

The point will perhaps become clearer when this approach is contrasted with the approach open to the theorist of characterization. In the context of the characterization question we define connections between persons and the actions, experiences, and characteristics which are theirs, and so the question, "Is this the person who committed the crime?" can be seen quite simply as the question, "Is this past action attributable to the person/subject we plan to punish?"[13] There is nothing in the form of the characterization

---

[13]On this view they are the same. That is the whole point; unlike the reidentification question, the characterization question does not force us to draw a distinction between person and subject.

question that prevents us from attributing past actions and experiences directly to present persons, and so providing them with a strong enough relation to those actions and experiences to justify our judgments of moral responsibility, self-interested concern, compensation, and survival.

A reidentification theorist may object to this analysis by saying that the phrasing of a question cannot in and of itself determine whether identity does or does not underlie the four features; only facts about the world can do so. In fact, such a theorist might continue, there is no deep connection between the different temporal moments of our lives, otherwise a reidentification theorist would be able to use this deep connection as the criterion of reidentification. I have, the objection would continue, merely asserted that it is possible to define a relationship between a person in the present and a past action or experience which is strong enough to underlie our attitudes concerning the four features. The extreme claim shows, however, that no such relation exists, and merely rephrasing the question, my imagined interlocutor might conclude, solves nothing.

To this objection my reply is twofold. First, although it is indeed true that the phrasing of a question cannot change facts about the world, it can obscure them or render them inexpressible. There may be a deep connection between the different parts of a person's life which can be expressed as a relation between a person and temporally distant actions, experiences, and character traits, but not as a relation between person time-slices. So far the only evidence we have that there is no deep unity throughout the course of a person's life is the inability of reidentification theorists to express one— the question of whether there *is* such a unity thus remains open until we have seen whether another approach fares better. Second, I acknowledge, of course, that I have so far given reasons for believing that it is possible only in the weakest sense to offer an account of characterization that avoids the extreme claim. Indeed, all I have shown is that this possibility is not ruled out by the form of this view as it is by the form of a reidentification criterion. I cannot say anything stronger until I have actually provided an account of characterization. At the very least, however, there is reason to hope that the importance of identity might be captured through an investigation of the characterization question.

Facts about personal identity seem to underlie the four features. Reidentification theorists assume this means that facts about *reidentification* underlie the four features and so try to capture this connection in a reidentification criterion for persons. My goal here has been to suggest that we should view the four features as attaching to facts about *characterization* and so look for insights into them within the context of the characterization question instead.

First of all, the assumption that the four features attach to identity in the sense investigated by the reidentification question has no particular presumption over the view I urge in its place—our original intuitions could just as easily be intuitions about characterization as about reidentification. Furthermore, in Part I I show that any attempt to capture the four features in a reidentification criterion for persons is doomed to failure by the very structure required of any such criterion—no relation having the appropriate logical structure to serve as a reidentification criterion can explain the link between the four features and identity. An attempt to capture this link in a view with the form of an answer to the characterization question, on the other hand, does not suffer these initial difficulties. The logical form of an account of characterization is in harmony with that of the four features, and because nothing in the form of this view precludes the attribution of temporally distant actions and experiences directly to presently existing psychological subjects, its form does not make it automatically vulnerable to the extreme claim.

That the form of the characterization question seems so much more like that of the relations that comprise the four features than the form of the reidentification question does gives us some prima facie reason to believe that the characterization question provides a much more appropriate context for considering these questions. At the very least, we know that it is not possible to capture these features with a theory of identity in the form of a reidentification criterion, but it just might be possible to do so with an account in the form of an answer to the characterization question. This alone seems ample reason to turn to the characterization question when we are interested in understanding this aspect of personal identity.

5

The Narrative Self-Constitution View

I call my response to the characterization question the narrative self-constitution view. It draws its inspiration from a number of sources both philosophical and psychological which argue either that persons are self-creating (this includes authors as diverse as Daniel Dennett, Jean-Paul Sartre, Harry Frankfurt, Jonathan Glover, and Martin Heidegger),[1] or that the lives of persons are narrative in form (this includes Alasdair MacIntyre in philosophy, and Donald Spence, Jerome Bruner, Roy Schafer, David Polonoff, and Mark Freeman in psychology).[2] Weaving strands from these discussions together with my own analysis, I develop a view according to which a person creates his identity by forming an autobiographical narrative—a story of his life.

Stated so baldly, the view may not sound very appealing—yet this approach provides a highly plausible account of personal identity which captures and illuminates the four features. Unlike the psychological continuity theory, this view can explain our intuitions about the relation between personal identity and survival, moral responsibility, self-interested concern, and compensation.

[1] See for instance, Daniel Dennett, *Elbow Room: The Varieties of Free Will Worth Wanting* (Cambridge: MIT Press, 1990), pp. 74-100; Jean-Paul Sartre, *Being and Nothingness* (New York: Washington Square Press, 1956); Frankfurt, "Identification and Externality," pp. 239-52; Jonathan Glover, *The Philosophy and Psychology of Personal Identity* (London: Penguin, 1988), pp. 131-38; and Martin Heidegger, *Being and Time* (New York: Harper and Row, 1962).

[2] See Alasdair MacIntyre, "The Virtues, the Unity of a Human Life, and the Concept of a Tradition," in Stanley Hauerwas and L. Gregory Jones, eds., *Why Narrative?* (Grand Rapids, Mich.: Wm. B. Eerdmans, 1989); Donald Spence, *Narrative Truth and Historical Truth* (New York: W. W. Norton, 1982); Jerome Bruner, *Actual Minds/Possible Worlds* (Cambridge: Harvard University Press, 1986), and *Acts of Meaning* (Cambridge: Harvard University Press, 1990); Roy Schafer, "Narration in the Psychoanalytic Dialogue," in W. J. T. Mitchell, ed., *On Narrative* (Chicago: University of Chicago Press, 1981); David Polonoff, "Self-Deception," *Social Research* 54 (1987); and especially, Mark Freeman, *Rewriting the Self: History, Memory, Narrative* (London: Routledge, 1993).

Basic Contours

The narrative self-constitution view starts from the relatively uncontroversial assumption that not all sentient creatures are persons. Personhood —at least insofar as it acts as the underpinning for moral agency, compensation, self-interested concern, and, I contend, survival—involves more than rudimentary consciousness. The narrative self-constitution view acknowledges a deep and intimate connection between personal identity and human identity but nonetheless follows such philosophers as Peter Strawson, Harry Frankfurt, Herbert Fingarette, and John Locke, who have variously argued for a distinction between human beings and persons, and between personal history and the history of a human body.[3]

According to the narrative self-constitution view, the difference between persons and other individuals (I use the word "individual" to refer to any sentient creature) lies in how they organize their experience, and hence their lives. At the core of this view is the assertion that individuals constitute themselves as persons by coming to think of themselves as persisting subjects who have had experience in the past and will continue to have experience in the future, taking certain experiences as theirs. Some, but not all, individuals weave stories of their lives, and it is their doing so which makes them persons. On this view a person's *identity* (in the sense at issue in the characterization question) is constituted by the content of her self-narrative, and the traits, actions, and experiences included in it are, by virtue of that inclusion, hers.

This claim constitutes the core of the narrative self-constitution view, but of course more must be added before it can provide a plausible account of personal identity. A view that held that *any* narrative self-conception was identity-constituting would be committed to the obviously false claim that persons cannot be mistaken about themselves. The narrative self-constitution view avoids this result by placing constraints on the kind of narrative that can constitute a person's identity. Only narratives that fall within these constraints are taken to be identity-defining, and what we commonly take to be mistakes in self-conception are, on this view, places where a person's self-narrative violates these constraints.

As we have just seen, the narrative self-constitution view has two major elements. The first is the claim that individuals constitute themselves as

---

[3]See Peter Strawson, "Freedom and Resentment," in G. Watson, ed., *Free Will* (Oxford: Oxford University Press, 1983); Frankfurt, "Freedom of the Will," pp. 81-95; Herbert Fingarette, *Self-Deception* (London, Routledge, 1969); and John Locke, "Of Identity and Diversity," in *Essay concerning Human Understanding*.

persons by creating self-narratives. The second is a set of limitations on the form of an identity-constituting narrative. The insights supporting each aspect of the view can be separated initially, but are, in the end, deeply intertwined.

The impetus for the view of persons as self-creating—and specifically as creating themselves through their self-conceptions—comes from the recognition that facts about an individual's subjective relation to her actions and experience is profoundly relevant to judgments of characterization and the four features. An identity in the sense of the characterization question, is not, I claim, something that an individual has whether she knows it or not, but something that she has *because* she acknowledges her personhood and appropriates certain actions and experiences as her own. Personhood and personal identity thus rely crucially on an individual's inner life and her attitude toward her actions and experiences. It is this fact which suggests that self-constitution must be part of a viable account of identity.

At the same time, however, it must be acknowledged that persons do not exist in a vacuum. The very concept of personhood is inherently connected to the capacity to take one's place in a certain complex web of social institutions and interactions—to act as a moral agent, enter into contracts, plan for one's future, express oneself and in general live the life of a person. Here I follow Wollheim's eloquent account of the importance of understanding the concept of living the life of a person to questions of personhood and personal identity.[4] What is characteristic of being a person is leading the life of a person; and in order to do this, one needs more than simply *any* concept of self, one needs a self-concept that is basically in synch with the view of one held by others. Personhood, it might be said, is an intrinsically social concept. To enter into the world of persons an individual needs, roughly speaking, to grasp her culture's concept of a person and apply it to herself. It is this recognition which leads to the constraints on an identity-constituting narrative—to be identity-defining an individual's self-narrative must conform in certain crucial respects to the narrative others tell of his life.

These, then, are the two basic sets of intuitions that lead to the narrative self-constitution view as I present it: first, that in order to be a person one needs a particular kind of subjectivity and orientation toward one's life, and second, that in order to be a person one's self-conception must cohere with what might be called the "objective" account of her life—roughly the story that those around her would tell.[5] These two aspects of identity are, how-

---

[4]See Wollheim, *The Thread of Life*, pp. 1–32.

[5]Obviously there is no single narrative which is *the* objective story of a person's life. Different people narrate a person's life in different ways, and so the "objective" narrative as I

ever, just different sides of the same coin. The kind of subjectivity required for personhood is precisely that necessary for the kinds of interactions definitive of personhood, and it is organizing one's self-conception according to these objectively determined constraints which generates that kind of subjectivity.

Narrative Form

The cornerstone of the narrative self-constitution view is the claim that a person's identity is created by a self-conception that is narrative in form. Most broadly put, this means that constituting an identity requires that an individual conceive of his life as having the form and the logic of a story—more specifically, the story of a person's life—where "story" is understood as a conventional, linear narrative. This broad characterization needs to be filled out in two ways. First, more must be said about the logic and form of the story of a person's life; and second, some justification must be given for demanding that an identity-constituting narrative have *this* form.

THE NATURE OF NARRATIVE FORM

Perhaps the most salient feature of narrative form in general is that the individual incidents and episodes in a narrative take their meaning from the broader context of the story in which they occur. Bruner nicely summarizes the element of narrative that is crucial here when he says, "A narrative is composed of a unique sequence of events, mental states, happenings involving human beings as characters or actors. These are its constituents. But these constituents do not, as it were, have a life or meaning of their own. Their meaning is given by their place in the overall configuration of the sequence as a whole—its plot or *fabula*."[6] MacIntyre applies this insight specifically to the lives of persons. He argues that the individual actions and experiences in a person's life cannot be understood outside the context of a biography, telling us that "successfully identifying and understanding what someone else is doing we always move towards placing a particular episode in the context of a set of narrative histories, histories both of the individuals concerned and of the settings in which they act and suffer," and that this is because "action itself has a basically historical character."[7]

---

use the term is not a monolith. All I mean to imply here is that there are certain basic constraints on a narrative which come from the publicly accessible facts about the history of an individual.

[6]Bruner, *Acts of Meaning*, pp. 43–44.
[7]MacIntyre, "The Virtues," p. 97.

To say that a person's life is narrative in character, then, is at least in part to claim that no time-slice (if you will) is fully intelligible—or even definable—outside the context of the life in which it occurs. To say that a person's *self-conception* is narrative is to say that she understands her own life in this way—interpreting the individual episodes in terms of their place in the unfolding story. A person's self-conception is a narrative self-conception, then, insofar as the incidents and experiences that make up his life are not viewed in isolation, but interpreted as part of the ongoing story that gives them their significance. In the next section I have a great deal more to say about what, in practical terms, it means to understand one's life in this way, but there is more that must still be said about the form of the self-conception required by the narrative self-constitution view. This view, after all, requires, not only that a person's self-conception take the form of a narrative, but more specifically that it take the form of the story of a person's life. This means that the logic by which the various parts of the narrative fit together is the logic associated with the unfolding of the life of a personal subject.

We expect a person's beliefs, desires, values, emotions, actions, and experiences to hang together in a way that makes what she says, does, and feels psychologically intelligible. The general gist of this observation can be captured by considering the distinction we recognize between fictional characters who are well drawn and those who are not. Sometimes the collection of actions, thoughts, emotions, and characteristics ascribed to a character make sense—we can understand her reactions, motivations, and decisions—they pull together to present a robust picture. Other times, however, we are at a loss to put together the information we are given about a character. Although each of the actions, emotions, beliefs, and so on that are ascribed to her may be unproblematic in itself, we have no sense of how to understand them as coexisting in a single subject—we get no sense of *who* this person is and what the guiding principles of her life are. A parallel distinction can be drawn in the case of biographical and autobiographical narratives. These are stories of lives, and the subjects of these stories can be well-defined characters or ill-defined ones, just as the protagonists of fictional narratives can be.

Roughly, then, the narrative self-constitution view requires that a person have a self-conception that coheres to produce a well-defined character. It should be obvious that this narrative can be intelligible to almost any degree. At one extreme there is the ideal (which no one actually attains) of perfect intelligibility—a life story in which every aspect coheres with every other. At the other extreme there is a random sequence of experiences that have little, if any, relation to one another. In between lie many possibilities—the narrative that is mostly intelligible with a few anomalous parts (the most common for persons), the conflicted story of the adolescent experiencing an identity crisis, or the disjointed story of the person with dementia.

The demand that a person's narrative be intelligible cannot, therefore, be a *categorical* demand, for intelligibility is not an all-or-nothing condition. Instead, this constraint manifests itself in two ways. First, the ideal of perfect intelligibility must be recognized *as* an ideal and respected as a demand on one's self-conception. To be a person one must realize that one's beliefs, desires, values, and traits are *supposed* to support one another. This involves acknowledging the legitimacy of certain kinds of questions and challenges—for example, "You've worked your whole life for this chance—why are you walking away from it now?" or "You say she's your best friend, why are you always so cruel to her?" or "You were always so quiet in High School—how did you ever end up as a lounge singer?" or "You said just the opposite yesterday; what's behind the turnaround?" In each case the question is a request to make intelligible a trait that seems anomalous or out of character. A person may not always be able to comply with such a request, but to have the right kind of self-conception one must at least recognize that it is legitimate, thereby showing a basic understanding of what the life story of a person *should* look like.

Second, in order for a narrative to be identity-constituting, it must have a high degree of coherence. There is, of course, no precise measure of how coherent an identity-constituting narrative must be—nor need there be such a measure. Personhood and attribution, like coherence, admit of degrees, and the degree of personhood and attribution varies with the degree to which a person's narrative coheres. This is true in two senses. First the degree to which a person's identity is well-defined overall depends on the degree of cohesiveness of his narrative as a whole. This fits nicely with our pre-philosophical intuitions—the more the different elements of a person's life hang together the more definite she is as a character, and so the better-defined her identity. Second, the more a particular action, experience, or characteristic coheres with the rest of a person's narrative (that is, the more in character it is), the greater the degree to which it contributes to the overall intelligibility of that narrative, and so the greater the degree to which it is attributable to him. A person's self-conception thus has the form of a story of a person's life to just the extent that it approximates the ideal of complete psychological intelligibility. This gives the fundamental idea of what is meant by the demand that a person's self-conception be narrative in form.

What remains is to provide some explanation of why the narrative self-constitution view makes this demand.

JUSTIFYING NARRATIVE FORM

It may seem, initially, that the demand that a person's self-conception take the form of a conventional narrative is unduly conservative and chauvinistic. The narrative self-constitution view seems to make the very strong (or at least very strong-sounding) claim that in order to be a *person* at all one must construct a narrative of this form. Although this view is not, in the end, quite so severe, it does insist on an approximation of traditional narrative form for an identity-constituting self-conception, and the justification for this requirement may not be obvious.

The general identification of narrative with conventional linear story form has been under attack from a number of quarters. Literary theorists, anthropologists, sociologists, and others have suggested that the assumption that a person's life and self-conception must follow the logic of a linear story is narrow and repressive. The goal of this section is to clear up some of the issues concerning narratives considered nonstandard from the point of view of our cultural mainstream and to offer reassurance that the narrative self-constitution view is neither as implausible nor as reactionary as it may at first appear. To do this it is important, first of all, to recall that the goal of the narrative self-constitution view is to capture the intuitive relation between personal identity and the four features. Persons are dramatically interested in their own survival and concerned for their own futures; they are moral agents and able to enter into relations of compensation. These attitudes and practices all seem linked to identity, and our immediate purpose is to define the concept of identity that underlies this link.

In the introduction to this chapter I explained that the narrative self-constitution view is based on the recognition that the practices we take to be definitive of the lives of persons depend on a certain self-conception. More particularly, a sentient individual must think about herself and her life in a certain way in order to bear the relation to the four features we have taken to be definitive of personhood. The defense of the demand for a traditional linear narrative as the form of an identity-constituting self-conception comes from the realization that it is this kind of self-conception that is necessary for the four features and much else involved in leading the life of a person. It is important to recognize, however, that this argument does not make any kind of categorical value judgment. Those whose self-conceptions take a form sufficiently different from our own cannot lead the kind of lives we live and will be excluded from certain kinds of interactions with us. They also have a different kind of subjectivity. This does not, however, mean that their lives are necessarily *inferior* to ours. "Person" is indeed an honorific, but it is only if one assumes that "non-personal" means the same as "subpersonal" that the denial of personhood is a *necessarily* negative evaluation.

The narrative self-constitution view thus holds firm on the claim that a self-conception sufficiently unlike a traditional linear narrative excludes personhood. The harsh sound of this claim is mitigated, however, in two ways. First, this view acknowledges that personhood is only one among many forms of existence, and although we, as persons, value our personhood, we do not need to insist that it is the only valuable form of existence. Second, the narrative self-constitution view recognizes that a number of different narrative styles fall under the category of a traditional linear narrative and so allows for a wide diversity of identity-constituting narratives.

With this general picture in hand, a look at some specific examples helps to clarify and support the narrative self-constitution view's insistence on linear narrative form. The intuitions at work are most easily seen in extreme cases. Consider first, then, the case of an individual whose self-conception is nothing whatsoever like a narrative—someone wholly lacking a *life story*. This sort of situation might occur, for instance, in someone who has achieved the satori-like dissolution of the self that Parfit sometimes seems to recommend. I do not pretend to be able to give an accurate picture of the complexities of the Buddhist view of the self here. For our purposes, however, the familiar, popularized version as read through Parfit will serve. What Parfit recommends, having discovered the superficiality of psychological continuation, is that we take seriously the Buddhist idea that the self is a fiction, and that enlightenment is to be achieved by coming to experience it as such. We should, he sometimes seems to argue, cease to think of ourselves as continuing and well-demarcated subjects and instead live in the moment, severing bonds with the past and the future. In the terms of psychological continuity theorists, this would involve each person time-slice recognizing itself for the independent entity that it is, and so failing to feel any sort of special connection to the other time-slices we judge to be part of the same person.

There is, of course, some disagreement about whether such a self-conception is achievable, but Parfit, who equates the Zen state of satori with a reductionist self-conception, comments that "Nagel once claimed that it is psychologically impossible to believe the Reductionist View. Buddha claimed that, though this is very hard, it is possible. I find Buddha's claim to be true."[8] Let us grant the possibility of this kind of self-conception for the sake of argument and ask about the individual who achieves it—an individual whose sentience is focused always in the present and never extends—either cognitively or affectively—to the past or future.[9]

It should be immediately obvious that individuals who arrange their experience in this way lead lives exceedingly different from our own. Such individuals do not make plans, engage in long-term commitments, or take responsibility for the past; their subjectivity and their actions are both quite different from our own. The differences between the kind of life led by an individual with a totally nonnarrative self-conception and the kind of life led by the rest of us are so pronounced and important that it does not seem like an exaggeration to say that the individuals who live such lives are not persons. This is, in fact, a conclusion endorsed by those who advocate such a self-conception. The purpose of trying to achieve satori is precisely to free oneself from concern about personal survival, anxiety about the future, remorse about the past, obsession with compensation—in other words, to dissolve and transcend personal existence. Parfit, too, recommends a change of self-conception as a means to overcoming the (to his mind) illusory concerns and attachments that are the natural result of how we now think about ourselves.

The narrative self-constitution view thus agrees with Parfit's claim that a radical change in psychological organization involving the renunciation of a narrative sense of self, in effect, dismantles the person. It differs from this claim (and related Buddhist views) on the question of whether the personal self is, therefore, a fiction. Parfit argues that the four features are never justified and the giving up of a narrative self-conception simply allows us to recognize that fact. The narrative self-constitution view holds that the kinds of connections between the different temporal portions of a person's life which provide a basis for the four features are *created* by the having of a self-conception. The basis for the four features is thus not illusory for individuals who have self-conceptions of the sort described in the narrative self-constitution view, but disappears when this self-conception does. It is in this sense that the narrative self-constitution view can hold that personhood is created by the creation of a narrative self-conception and that individuals with nonnarrative senses of self are not persons. It should again be noted

---

[8]Parfit, *Reasons and Persons*, p. 280.

[9]This condition is, of course, hard even to describe. The mere need to talk about such an "individual" already seems to deny the reality of punctuality. The difficulty of formulation does not, however, undermine the position, as the Buddhist can argue that it is a poverty of our language and conceptual scheme which prevents a better formulation.

that this claim remains agnostic concerning the superiority of one mode of existence over the other.

Charges of chauvinism against the narrative self-constitution view based on its denial of personhood to individuals who have *no* kind of narrative structure to their experience at all are thus misplaced. Thinking of oneself as persisting through time and of the different temporal parts of one's existence as being mutually influential is a minimal requirement of the state we call personhood. There are, however, many cases less extreme than this—cases where an individual has some sort of narrative or story of his life, but not a traditional, linear narrative. All of the stretching and redefining of narrative that is possible in literature, it seems, might occur in an individual's self-conception, and so many alternative narrative forms are possible. Moreover, there have been a number of suggestions that in fact alternate conceptions of the self *are* widespread among nondominant elements of the culture and that the emphasis on a linear narrative conception as the standard of what a life story should look like is a form of repression. It might thus appear that insistence on this kind of narrative as definitive of personal identity is a way of insisting on conformity to the worldview of dominant groups.

It is difficult to offer a general response to worries about moderately alternative narrative forms because there are so many different cases to consider. There are virtually countless alternatives to the standard conception of narrative, each of which bears a different relation to the narrative self-constitution view and so raises a slightly different set of questions. It is, of course, impossible to address each conceivable alternative on its own, but I can extract some general themes that provide a sense of how the narrative self-constitution view deals with a wide range of alternate narrative styles.

The first thing to realize is that an alternative narrative might deviate from the standard form to almost any degree, but in most cases, there is a great deal of overlap between a conventional narrative and an avant-garde alternative. Most of the ways in which our conception of narrative is stretched or redefined are variations on the traditional conception that play with one or more features. What this means is that although some experimental narratives bear little or no resemblance to what we think of as a story, for the most part there are more similarities than differences between alternative narratives and standard linear ones.

A second fact to bear in mind while considering non-mainstream narratives is that differences in narrative style usually produce differences in subjectivity and in the capacity to engage in the kinds of activities and practices definitive of personhood. This is particularly clear with respect to the four features—conceptions of responsibility, survival, concern, and compensation vary with the kind of narrative one tells. Indeed, recognition of this correspondence underlies the political force associated with challenges to traditional conceptions of narrative. It is at least in part because it is assumed that a different conception of the limits of the self or the logic of a life leads to correspondingly different judgments concerning the four features that the privileging of the standard linear narrative is taken to be problematically chauvinistic.

A great deal of work in feminist ethics and political philosophy, for instance, argues that the views of morality, agency, and self-interest that underlie conventional philosophical discussion come from exclusive attention to a traditional conception of the self that leaves out the kinds of narratives more natural to women and to persons from non-Anglo-European cultures. The clear implication is that our judgments concerning the four features would be different if we operated with a different conception of what constitutes the story of a person's life. This, in turn, suggests that the four features and other aspects definitive of the lives of persons are linked to the form of one's self-conception. The call for tolerance for different narrative styles and the different social organizations and moral judgments that go with them is thus at the same time a recognition of the link between the form of one's self-conception and the four features.

Not only is there an acknowledged link between narrative style and the four features, but for the most part the degree to which an individual's sense of the four features is nonstandard in our culture corresponds to the degree to which the form of her self-narrative is nonstandard. The self-conception of an extreme psychotic, for instance, is likely to differ from our standard conception of narrative far more than that of someone from another culture, or from a subculture within this culture. Correspondingly, the ability to enter into the attitudes and practices we take to make up the life of a person are severely compromised in the case of the psychotic, whereas they are probably affected only subtly in the case of the individual whose self-conception merely contains a different narrative spin.

From these observations we can draw some general morals that help clarify the claims of the narrative self-constitution view. First, it seems clear that this view needs to allow for a somewhat vague and fluid idea of a "standard" narrative. Even calling for a traditional linear conception, there is no *single* form that the story of a person's life must take, but rather a cluster of narrative forms that overlap in large part and differ in some particulars. To take a somewhat caricatured example, it may turn out that in general women tend to employ a more cyclical notion of time in their narratives than men do, or to draw the boundaries between self and other a little less sharply. The narrative self-constitution view should not be taken to imply that we must decide that either men or women have "nonstandard" narratives and so are not fully persons. Rather, this view can allow these quite similar, but still distinct, narrative styles as types of standard narrative.

At some point, the deviation of an individual's self-conception from the range of narratives standard in our culture can be so great that comprehension of and interaction with such individuals becomes difficult. This is the sort of divergence that can often be found in cases of extreme cultural difference. In such a case the narrative self-constitution view might recognize that this culture has persons, but also note that their concept of persons—and so the persons themselves—are quite different from in our culture. For instance, a tribal culture might assign to an ancestral lineage much of the role that the individual person plays in our culture—responsibility, for instance, may be felt most directly for all of the actions of an ancestral line rather than for the actions of the individual alone, and self-interested and survival concerns may also be primarily attached to the lineage. Presumably the members of this culture would also recognize what we call a single person as a natural unit, but this unit would play a different role in their interactions and practices.

This difference in social organization, it may be assumed, will lead to a difference in individual psychological organization, which will in turn affect the capacities and subjectivity of the members of that culture. Most likely, if this is a human culture, there will be sufficient overlap between their worldview and ours to allow the kind of fundamental similarities that lead us to recognize it as a culture of persons. We are unlikely to run into an actual tribe of functioning human beings whose lives and psychologies are so differently organized from our own that they do not seem to be persons at all—indeed recent work in evolutionary psychology suggests that there may be sound scientific rationale for assuming something like a fundamentally universal human nature. Still, there can be enough variation for another culture to appear terribly alien, and in a case like this, unlike the already-described cases involving minor differences, the narrative self-constitution view would say that although this culture has persons, their conception of persons is different from our own.

The narrative self-constitution view thus allows a broad range of divergence in identity-constituting narrative styles. A family of mostly overlapping narrative forms and the practices that go with them count, for our purposes, as standard life stories, and so as the kind of narratives that unproblematically constitute a person in our sense of the word. Narrative styles outside this family group which retain certain of its most basic features also constitute persons, but persons unlike us. When a self-conception becomes wildly different in form from those standard in our culture—for example, a self-conception that is not even narrative in form—the narrative self-constitution view does not consider it identity-constituting at all, nor those who organize their experience in this way persons. The question of just *how* different a narrative must be before it is removed from the family of narratives making up the standard form, or is ruled out as identity-constituting altogether, is largely an empirical one. Some of the most brilliant moments in fiction are achieved by those who expand our perception of what kind of thing can be a comprehensible story, and the most brilliant lives may do the same.

The narrative self-constitution view thus demands that a person's self-conception take the form of a traditional linear narrative because it is this kind of self-conception which underlies the attitudes and practices that define the life of a person. This view allows that a range of narrative styles can count as standard and also recognizes the possibility of conceptions of persons different from our own, but insists that a self-narrative that deviates sufficiently from the form of a conventional story does not constitute a person or create a personal identity.

Having a Narrative

The previous section described the form that an identity-constituting self-conception must have according to the narrative self-constitution view. It may seem questionable, however, whether anyone really has such a self-conception. The formal construction of an autobiography is no easy task, and there is no reason to believe that all—or even most—persons ever undertake it. Although persons are often self-reflective, and sometimes make a self-conscious effort to understand where they have come from, where they are going, and how the parts of their lives fit together, most often they simply live. The demand of a fully written autobiography that one, so to speak, "carries in one's head" is obviously far too stringent a prerequisite for personhood. The narrative self-constitution view does not, of course, make this demand—the construction of an identity-constituting autobiographical narrative does not have to be self-conscious.

We can begin to get a sense of what is involved in having an identity-constituting self-narrative by looking at Locke's work on personal identity. Locke provides an insight that yields a plausible understanding of how persons create an autobiographical sense of self. My discussion of Locke's text focuses almost exclusively on the chapter of the *Essay concerning Human Understanding* titled "Of Identity and Diversity." This discussion is not a work of Locke scholarship. My primary interest here is not to uncover Locke's own intentions, but to pull a strand from his text which puts us on the path toward developing a successful account of characterization.[10]

Although this aspect of Locke's discussion of identity is rarely emphasized, it seems clear that he is a self-constitution theorist. In discussing which actions and experiences belong to a particular person, Locke often says that it is those which the person *appropriates*,[11] thus pointing to the active role persons play in defining their own identities. Even more explicitly, he tells us that "person" stands for "a thinking intelligent Being, that has reason and reflection, and can consider it self as it self, the same thinking thing in different times and places,"[12] and adds later that "where-ever a Man finds, what he calls *himself*, there I think another may say is the same *Person*."[13]

This leads immediately to the question of what it is, on Locke's view, for someone to take herself to be the same thinking thing at different times and places, or to appropriate a particular action or experience as her own. To answer this question, we should first return to that part of Locke's view which *has* received a great deal of attention—his claim that personal identity is constituted by sameness of consciousness. He says, for instance, that "as far as this consciousness can be extended backwards to any past Action or Thought, so far reaches the Identity of that *Person*";[14] and that "as far as any intelligent Being can repeat the *Idea* of any past Action with the same consciousness it had of it at first, and with the same consciousness it has of any present Action; so far it is the same *personal self*."[15] He says further that

---

[10]I think it is important to develop this insight via Locke's text for two reasons: First, I believe it is really there. Second, and most important, Locke is almost universally taken to provide the first psychological continuity theory and to provide the canonical expression of the considerations supporting a psychological account of personal identity. If it turns out, as I claim, that Locke's words can be seen to be addressing the characterization question instead of the reidentification question, my original claim that personal identity theorists suffer from applying the Lockean insight to the wrong identity question will have that much more credibility.

[11]He says, for instance, "For as to this point of being the same *self*, it matters not whether this present *self* be made up of the same or other Substances, I being as much concern'd, and as justly accountable for any Action was done a thousand Years since, appropriated to me now by this self-consciousness, as I am, for what I did the last moment." Locke, *An Essay concerning Human Understanding*, p. 341.

[12]Ibid., p. 335.

[13]Ibid., p. 346.

[14]Ibid., p. 335.

[15]Ibid., p. 336.

"this may shew us wherein *personal Identity* consists, not in the Identity of Substance, but, as I have said, in the Identity of *consciousness*."[16] Similar pronouncements can be found throughout Locke's discussion.

The claim that personal identity is constituted by sameness of consciousness requires interpretation. Locke's critics are quick to point out the obscurity of phrases like "extending consciousness backwards in time," "repeating an idea with the same consciousness as of present actions," or "sameness of consciousness." Reid explicitly considers the question of what these could mean and concludes that Locke must be talking about memory connections. He says, "Mr. Locke attributes to consciousness the conviction we have of our past actions, as if a man may now be conscious of what he did twenty years ago. It is impossible to understand the meaning of this, unless by consciousness be meant memory, the only faculty by which we have an immediate knowledge of our past actions."[17] This reading has become standard, and it is common to view Locke as holding a memory theory of personal identity.

Trying to understand Locke in this way leaves us, however, with the nagging question of why he never *says* that memory connections constitute personal identity if this is what he means. He certainly has the concept of memory—he has an extended discussion of it in book 2, chapter 10, of the *Essay*, and he uses the word "memory" many times in his discussion of personal identity. Indeed, it seems clear that he sees *some* connection between memory and personal identity. Nonetheless, when he tells us what personal identity consists in, which he does many times throughout the chapter, he *always* talks about extension of consciousness and *never* about memory connections.

There have been some attempts to provide an alternative understanding of "identity of consciousness" or "extension of consciousness," but in the end they are not much more satisfying than the memory theory. Noonan, for instance, argues that in seventeenth-century English, there were two meanings of "consciousness"—the first very like the modern meaning, and the second a stronger sense, implying shared knowledge. He takes Locke to be talking about consciousness in the latter sense, and says that on this understanding, "when one is 'conscious to oneself' knowledge of some-

---

[16]Ibid., p. 342. It is also interesting to note that in the quotations cited in notes 14 and 15 Locke makes it clear that his concern is with the ascription of particular actions and experiences to a particular person. This is, of course, the characterization question, not the reidentification question. On the other hand, the quotation cited here has a locution better suited to the reidentification question, so it is hard to know what to say here.

[17]Thomas Reid, "Of Mr. Locke's Account," p. 115.

thing is shared with oneself alone. In this use of the expression one may be thought of as a witness to one's own acts. Consciousness in the sense of 'consciousness to oneself,' then, is knowledge of oneself, knowledge of one's own thoughts and actions."[18] Being conscious to oneself of some past action is thus, on this view, sharing knowledge of that action with oneself alone, and it is in this that extension of consciousness consists.

This reading initially seems more promising than Reid's; it not only explains the absence of the term "memory" from Locke's theory of personal identity, it also highlights Locke's emphasis on the importance of *self-consciousness*. The implications of this reading, however, show that it is not much different from the memory theory in the end. Noonan explains: "Primarily, then, when Locke says that personal identity consists in sameness of consciousness he means that it consists in shared knowledge—the knowledge shared by the present and past self. Of course, the only knowledge we have of the past which is relevant to Locke's discussion is memory knowledge. Reid gets this absolutely right."[19] Although this reading has some advantages over Reid's, it still leaves us wondering why Locke would so thoroughly obscure his intended meaning.

Noonan's collapse of his stronger notion of "consciousness" into memory underscores the reasons we are likely to get stuck in trying to come up with an acceptable explication, and also points to the place in Locke where the resources to dig ourselves out can be found. Noonan, like Reid, cannot think of anything but memory that consciousness of the past could be because he, like Reid, is focusing exclusively on the cognitive aspects of consciousness. Consciousness is thought of as a faculty of *knowing*, and this makes the interpretation of consciousness of the past as memory almost irresistible.

This is not, however, the aspect of consciousness that Locke most emphasizes in his discussion of personal identity. Instead he stresses the *affective* side of consciousness. He paints a picture of consciousness as the faculty whereby we experience pleasure and pain, happiness and misery. He tells us, for instance, that "*Self* is that conscious thinking thing, (whatever Substance, made up of whether Spiritual, or Material, Simple, or Compounded, it matters not) which is sensible, or conscious of Pleasure and Pain, capable of Happiness or Misery, and so is concern'd for it *self* as far as that consciousness extends,"[20] thus emphasizing the definition of identity in terms of sameness of consciousness precisely because it is in consciousness that

---

[18]Noonan, *Personal Identity*, p. 53.
[19]Ibid., p. 54.
[20]Locke, *Essay concerning Human Understanding*, p. 341.

we experience the affect that underlies self-interested concern, compensation, and justice of punishment.

He draws a connection between the affective aspects of consciousness and the appropriation of particular actions and experiences when he tells us what makes a particular body (in the present) one's own. He says that the particles of one's body, "whilst vitally united to this same thinking conscious self, so that we feel when they are touch'd, and are affected by, and conscious of good or harm that happens to them, are a part of our *selves: i.e.* of our thinking conscious *self*. Thus the Limbs of his Body is to every one a part of *himself*: He sympathizes and is concerned for them."[21] It is, then, the fact that someone experiences what happens to certain bits of matter—that their condition directly affects him in the dimension of pleasure and pain—that makes them part of his consciousness, and so makes them his. The same, Locke says, is true of immaterial substance. It is insofar as someone is immediately caused pleasure or pain by the present states of a particular soul that that soul is, presently, hers.

This tells us how certain *present* experiences become part of present consciousness, but what of past experiences, how are we to think about extending consciousness backward in time? Locke offers a fairly simple answer. He tells us, "this personality extends it *self* beyond present Existence to what is past, only by consciousness, whereby it becomes concerned and accountable, owns and imputes to it *self* past Actions, *just upon the same ground, and for the same reason*, that it does the present."[22] Present actions are made part of a person's present consciousness by affecting his well-being or causing him pleasure or pain. Locke tells us that persons make past actions and experiences theirs on just the same grounds, so on his view past actions and experiences become those of a present person if they affect *present* consciousness, causing the person pleasure and pain in the *present*. On this reading we extend consciousness back in time to some past action or experience by caring about it in the appropriate way—by *feeling* its effects.

It is not difficult to see how past actions and experiences could cause present pleasure or pain. When someone is, at present, tortured by guilt or warmed by happy memories, or when she measures her current successes by comparison with past ones, past experiences are affecting her present well-being. This may appear, at first, to be just another incarnation of the memory theory. In the examples I gave it is the *memory* of some past event that causes the affect, and so it may seem that even on this view extending

[21]Ibid., pp. 336–37.
[22]Ibid., p. 346, my emphasis.

consciousness backward in time may come down to memory after all. There is, however, more to the story. It may be that in many cases our emotion concerning past actions and experiences is evoked by memories of those actions and experiences, but at least since Freud we have also known that the past can affect present well-being without being explicitly remembered. This can happen in a variety of ways. It is well-established, for instance, that individuals can repress explicit memory of particular experiences and yet feel associated emotions. There is evidence, for instance, that victims of severe trauma can sometimes lose cognitive memory of the details of the trauma and yet suffer depression and other affective disorders later in life. More common, less dramatic incidents (such as being humiliated by one's parents or schoolmates) may be forgotten and yet leave undeniable affective traces.

A repressed past can thus affect present consciousness without being remembered, but this is not the only mechanism by which the past can influence present consciousness without direct memory. Sometimes it is not specific events but rather global characteristics of the past that condition the present. To get a sense of what I mean by this, consider first an example in the present. Whether or not a person feels financially secure may have a broad-ranging impact on his emotions, actions, and way of living. A person who has enough money to feel secure that his needs will be provided for may not spend much time consciously reflecting on that fact, but perhaps he will feel no hesitation in making major purchases, be inclined to indulge himself when he sees something he wants, or allow his choices concerning his career to be motivated by considerations of personal fulfillment rather than compensation. He will, furthermore, not spend time obsessing about money; he will not get headaches from financial woes, and so on.

On the other hand, a person who does not feel financially secure may well have a much different attitude toward the transactions of everyday life. She may be racked with anxiety about major purchases, researching her options carefully and making sure she is getting the best price; she may indulge herself only in ways that do not involve spending extra money, or forfeit fulfillment in a career in favor of security; and become obsessive about or manifest somatic symptoms because of money worries. Of course, a person may respond to either wealth or poverty in a wide variety of ways, and these cases are meant only as examples. The point I am trying to make is that the effects of financial security are not easily cashed out in terms of occurrent mental states, or even in terms of dispositions to behave. Being financially secure is a way one addresses life—it provides a backdrop that affects the quality of almost all of one's day-to-day experience.

To make the point relevant to our reading of Locke, we need only see that it is often one's past financial status, rather than one's current circumstances, that determines whether or not one feels financially secure. On the one hand, a person raised in the lap of luxury may find it hard to adjust to a reversal of fortune and continue to indulge himself and make career choices as if he did not need to worry about financial considerations. On the other hand, people are fond of stories of relatives raised during the Depression who, although quite well off now, continue to hoard pieces of string or go miles out of their way to save a few pennies. The past, then, is able to affect the future in this global way—by conditioning the quality of a person's daily life. It can, furthermore, do so without being mediated through any specific memories—the string-saver need not have available to her any particular episode of hunger or deprivation when she decides to walk in the bitter cold rather than spend money on a cab. Granted, this person will probably remember several such episodes, and these memories will likely be at least part of what conditions present experience. There is no absurdity, however, in imagining that such a person could suffer some kind of amnesia in which she forgets all particular episodes of her past and yet retains the traits of thrift and financial conservatism that it has caused.

The kind of general effect the past can have on the future can be seen even more clearly when instead of the somewhat limited case of financial security we consider the even more general case of personal security or feelings of worthiness and self-esteem. It is no great revelation that a person who feels loved and valued by a stable family in childhood is more likely to grow up feeling worthy, entitled, and secure than a person who is made to feel worthless and incompetent. The general orientation toward the world of the former person—his interactions with others, his choices about what to do, his ability to weather setbacks and disappointments, and so on—is likely to be very different from that of the second, who is likely to be more timid, sensitive, and vulnerable.

I should stress here that I do not want to imply any kind of strict psychological determinism. What I am trying to emphasize by looking at these quite general ways in which the past can condition the present is that our pasts give us something besides particular memories. They also give us a "script"—a sense of self, an idea of who we are and what kind of story we are living. The well-nurtured child grows up to view herself as a person who will have a good life, and this affects how she acts, what she expects, and how she experiences the world. The person who is raised to view himself as a loser, however, will have a quite different experience of even the same sorts of episodes.

This, then, is how Locke's insight can be used to yield a helpful understanding of what is involved in having a narrative self-conception. Locke points out that past events can become part of present consciousness by affecting us in the present along the dimension of pleasure or pain. This can happen in a straightforward way—as when some memory causes guilt or remorse—but it can also happen in a more subtle way, by contributing to a person's overall sense of self. Our pasts give us our conception of who we are and what life story we are living, and this conception may well intensify or mitigate present emotion. The person, convinced by beatings and parental disapproval that the only thing that can make her worthwhile is to excel in athletic competition may well suffer much more intensely in losing, and be willing to go to far greater lengths to win, than the person who has come to believe that his athletic talent is just one of the many wonderful and lovable things about him, and that his life has many other rewards and adventures in store. To have a narrative self-conception on the view I am urging is thus to experience the events in one's life as interpreted through one's sense of one's own life story, and to feel the affect that follows upon doing so.

It is worth pointing out that although the discussion has focused on how the past influences present experience, Locke seems to imply (and I certainly want to say) that the future does so as well. We cannot, of course, remember the future, but we can anticipate it, and specific anticipations can often affect the quality of present experience. The graduate student struggling by on virtually no money may well almost enjoy the period as a romantic rite of passage; she can tell herself a story in which she is struggling toward membership in the ancient and honorable society of scholars. A father who has just landed below the poverty level again after thinking he was finally on his feet is, however, likely to experience that poverty quite differently; his story may well be one of repeated failure and frustration.

One last example sums up many of the themes we have so far explored. It comes from a fictional narrative—the movie *Now Voyager* with Bette Davis and Paul Henried.[23] In the film Charlotte Vale (Bette Davis) has been transformed by Dr. Joquith's (Claude Rains) miraculous treatment from the stocky, unattractive and highly neurotic spinster aunt of a wealthy New England family into a delightful, slim, and attractive woman. She takes a South American cruise to "try her wings" and on board begins a friendship

[23]Again I thank Stanley Cavell for introducing me to this movie, and for impressing upon me the importance of both the film itself, and this particular incident.

THE NARRATIVE SELF-CONSTITUTION VIEW

with the unhappily married Jerry (Paul Henried). As their intimacy grows she tries to help him understand her better by showing him a photograph of her somber family. Pointing to the photo he asks, "Who is the fat lady with the heavy brows and all the hair?" The significance of this story for present purposes comes from Charlotte/Bette Davis's reply: "I'm the fat lady with the heavy brows and all the hair."

This response speaks volumes. She does not tell him that she has a past self who was a fat lady with bushy eyebrows and more hair, nor that she has a past time-slice who was fat with lots of hair and eyebrows, nor even that she *was* the fat lady with the heavy brows and all the hair. Although she is no longer fat and has plucked her eyebrows, she *is* the fat lady with the hair and brows. What does this mean? It means, of course, that she *identifies* with the woman in the picture. But what does *that* amount to? Well, in this case it means that a particular significance has been bestowed on her cruise, and on her relationship with Jerry, that would not have existed if she were not the fat lady with the hair and brows. She feels exhilarated, frightened, proud, and somewhat fraudulent in the way she does because she knows where she has come from and how she got there. Her story is not the story of the always-beloved, but the story of the sorry caterpillar who has suddenly become a beautiful butterfly; these are two different stories, and it is something quite different to live the one rather than the other. Charlotte undoubtedly remembers her past all too well, but she does more than just remember it, she lives it—experiencing the present and planning the future in its light.

This discussion has shown us not only what besides the explicit telling of one's life story might be involved in having a narrative self-conception, but also that the telling of an explicit story is, indeed, usually an inappropriate way of expressing one's self-conception. The sense of one's life as unfolding according to the logic of a narrative is not just an *idea* we have, it is an organizing principle of our lives. It is the lens through which we filter our experience and plan for actions, not a way we think about ourselves in reflective hours. How we appropriate actions and experiences to make them part of our consciousness is thus much more like how we appropriate elements of food to make them parts of our bodies than how we appropriate books to make them part of our library. (Perhaps this is something like what Augustine had in mind when he called memory the "stomach of the mind.")[24] To have an autobiographical narrative in the relevant sense is thus to have an implicit understanding of one's history as unfolding according to the logic of the story of a person's life. With this deeper understanding of what it is for an individual to have a narrative self-conception of the form described in the previous section, we can now turn to a discussion of the further constraints the narrative self-constitution view puts on identity-constituting narrative.

The Articulation Constraint

Having an autobiographical narrative does not involve actually articulating the story of one's life to oneself or anyone else, but only organizing experience according to an implicit narrative. Nonetheless, the narrative self-constitution view does not allow a person's self-narrative to remain entirely subterranean. A further requirement is that an identity-constituting narrative be capable of local articulation. This means that the narrator should be able to explain why he does what he does, believes what he believes, and feels what he feels.

The sense of explanation at work in this constraint is a very ordinary one. In day-to-day intercourse we take it for granted that people are able to answer questions about themselves. Even those people who do not spend much time reflecting on their motivations can, in most cases, produce them when challenged. To take a very simple case, a grown man may not even notice that he looks both ways before he crosses the street, and almost certainly he does not think explicitly about *why* he does so, but if asked, he could probably answer without hesitation that he does not wish to be hit by a car. The same kind of presumption of explicability holds in just the same way in more complex cases. If, for instance, I ask the person who was torn between two jobs why she chose the one she did, I expect an explanation in terms of her long-term goals, personality traits, talents, likes, and dislikes. Similarly, if I ask someone why he was so upset about a seemingly trivial incident, I expect him to be able to answer in terms, perhaps, of his history and particular sensitivities. A person usually can, that is, account for her actions and experiences by showing how they are a part of an intelligible life story with a comprehensible and well-drawn subject as its protagonist. (It should go without saying that this presumption applies in just the same way for questions people ask themselves about their own conduct.)

The demand that an identity-constituting narrative be articulable, like the demand for linear narrative form, relies on the requirement that this feature of narrative self-conception explain the four features and yield the kind of subjectivity that allows for the life of a person. Before spelling out the justification for this constraint, however, it must be acknowledged that the constraint of articulation raises a number of difficult questions for the narrative self-constitution view. Although for the most part persons can account for their actions, emotions, and thoughts, they cannot *always* do so, and even in those cases where accounts are offered they are not always accurate.

It is not uncommon for us to be at a loss to explain some particular action or affective response. Sometimes emotions or impulses seem to come out of the blue, subverting the order and intelligibility of our lives—we often cannot explain our self-destructive behavior, or why we are leaving our partners, or where we find the strength to stand up for our rights, or why we are so undone by trivial disappointments. There are cases where we simply *cannot* tell some parts of our life stories in a way that makes them intelligible. Moreover, even when we do have ready accounts of our actions, it is sometimes all too obvious that our stories are inaccurate—a commonsense observation given formal expression, in different ways, by both Freudian and Cognitive psychology.

A man may, for instance, swear that he feels nothing but affection for his brother and explain the many instances in which he has hurt or undermined his brother as unfortunate accidents or slips following on the best intentions; or a woman may explain her job choice in terms of retirement benefits or advancement opportunities when it is obvious to those around her that she is rationalizing her decision to stay close to her no-good boyfriend. A number of empirical studies have shown, moreover, that even in cases that are not affectively charged our reasons for believing what we do may well be quite different from what we take them to be.

Given that the narrative self-constitution view includes the articulation constraint, it is necessary to explain what this view says about attribution and identity in cases where we have difficulty articulating our stories. Before turning to this explanation, I should clarify my terminology. I call instances of self-blindness (such as those I have just described) cases in which a person's *explicit* self-narrative diverges from his *implicit* self-narrative. The implicit narrative is understood as the psychological organization from which his experience and actions are actually flowing. It may not be obvious why I want to call this unarticulated (and sometimes unarticulable) psychological organization a *self*-narrative at all. The person explicitly denies the features we are attributing to her, and so it may seem perverse to say that they are part of her self-conception—even her implicit self-conception. It is, therefore, worth taking a bit of time to explain what my choice of terms is meant to emphasize.

I call a person's underlying psychological organization a *self*-narrative because it is not simply a static set of facts about him, but rather a dynamic set of organizing principles, a basic orientation through which, with or without conscious awareness, an individual understands himself and his world. These implicit organizing principles are not simply a collection of features, but a continually developing interpretation of the course of one's trajectory through the world. In this way it is legitimate to think of what I am calling the implicit self-narrative as a *self*-conception, even though it contains elements that the person explicitly denies.

Consider a common case of repression or self-deception—the aforementioned case of the man who fails to recognize the hostility he feels toward his brother will do nicely. In imagining a case like this we think of someone who sincerely insists that he feels nothing but respect and love for his brother, but nonetheless frequently behaves toward him in ways that suggest hostility—he may "forget" his brother's birthday, "unwittingly" serve his least favorite foods when inviting him to dinner, "inadvertently" say things that humiliate him, and so on. We may imagine further that he and his brother were always in competition for scarce resources—college money, parental affection—and that the brother routinely came out better. When these incidents are pointed out to our imagined subject, he protests that his actions are trivial accidents, and that we are making far too much of them.

Although hostility is not part of this man's explicit self-conception, it is clear that it plays a role in shaping his experience, actions, and emotions. Indeed, this is precisely why we confidently ascribe to him a hostility he denies. Even though his explicit account of his actions does not include phrases like "I hate my brother," the assumption that an underlying hostility is playing a role in constituting his experience and directing his actions is required to make sense of those explicit features of his life. We attribute unconscious affect and motivations to people when their actions and emotions can only be made intelligible by doing so. Although the hostility is not part of the story this person *tells* of himself, then, it can still be part of his self-conception in a very real way.

As has already been noted, however, people actually *narrate* very little of their lives in any self-conscious way. Instead, they permit a general set of background assumptions about themselves and their lives to guide the unfolding of experience. Indeed, constraints of time and the exigencies of life make it impossible to articulate full life narratives, and so explicitness cannot be a prerequisite for an element's being part of a person's self-conception. Granted, there is a deeply significant difference between those unstated elements which *are* easily available to the subject and those which are not—a difference that has serious implications for personal identity. Still, I wish to maintain that insofar as both kinds of elements shape the way a person approaches the world they are both part of her self-narrative.

I realize that this is a somewhat unusual way to think about "self-narrative," and that I may not have satisfied everyone that it is a legitimate one. In the end, however, very little really turns on this choice of words. It does not matter much whether we say that identity is determined by a person's self-narrative or by his psychical organization, so long as it is understood that the psychological forces constituting identity are dynamic and active—things a person *does*—rather than static and passive features she *has*. I use the term "self-narrative," even though it is somewhat controversial here, to underscore these features of a person's psychological life.

The question of what the narrative self-constitution view says about identity and attribution in those cases where implicit and explicit narratives diverge, however, still remains to be addressed. The articulation constraint described at the opening of this section seems to imply that if there is some part of an individual's narrative that he cannot explicate, the narrative as a whole fails to be identity-constituting. This interpretation is obviously too extreme—it would have the consequence that any individual who is at all self-blind would fail to constitute herself as a person, and that cannot be right. The articulation constraint should thus not be taken to require absolute transparency. Instead, it acknowledges that the elements of a person's narrative he cannot articulate are his, but says that they are only partially his—attributable to him to a lesser degree than those aspects of the narrative he can articulate. It implies, moreover, that if the inability to articulate one's narrative is sufficiently widespread and severe, the overall degree of personhood can also be compromised.

Our earlier discussion has shown why the narrative self-constitution view needs to allow that unarticulated aspects of a person's implicit self-narrative are at least partially hers. These elements do play a role in the person's life, affecting action and experience, and must be attributed to her to make her actions and emotions intelligible. What requires a bit more explanation is the sense in which the elements of a person's narrative he cannot articulate are less fully his than those he can. At first it might seem as if our intuitions run quite to the contrary—we feel that emotions and desires lurking deep in someone's unconscious are *more* definitive of who she *really* is than those she can easily explicate. The psychological elements that make it to a person's consciousness have, after all, gone through a process of censorship devised, at least in part, to protect him from some of the more painful truths about himself. The official versions of our histories are thus much sanitized, and it is tempting to believe that the *real* story is the one not told.

This intuition is certainly legitimate and should not be ignored. Still, it cannot be denied that at the same time there is another sense in which it is perfectly natural and intuitive to say that the repressed or unconscious elements of a person's implicit narrative are less fully her own than those of which she is aware. Those features of one's life which cannot be articulated do play a role, but they play a role different from that played by those which can be. They are not subject to the same kind of scrutiny as are narrative features of which the person can become aware and are not, therefore, as well integrated into his life, which restricts the form their expression can take.

Because unconscious elements are part of a person's implicit narrative they do influence emotion and action, but because they are hidden from view their influence is rigid and automatic. Freud describes the character of such influence in his discussion of the bedtime rituals of an obsessive patient. He says that in carrying out these rituals, "she behaved in precisely the same way as a hypnotized subject whom Bernheim had ordered to open an umbrella in the hospital ward five minutes after he woke up. The man carried out this instruction when he was awake, but he could produce no motive for his actions."[25] The analogy to posthypnotic suggestion is important. It underscores just how strongly alienated a person is from her unconscious impulses and the actions that carry them out. These impulses, Freud says, "give the patient himself the impression of being all-powerful guests from an alien world, immortal beings intruding into the turmoil of mortal life."[26]

This analysis shows the sense in which we feel that the elements of a person's narrative she cannot explicate are less fully her own than those she can. It also shows why widespread or serious failure to be able to explicate one's narrative can be seen to compromise the overall degree of personhood. Insofar as unconscious features are elements of a person's narrative, they have an effect on the actions and experiences of which she is aware; insofar as they are unconscious, these effects are mysterious to the narrator. When a person is unable to explicate part of her narrative, some set of her actions and experiences are incomprehensible to her and, hence, not properly under her control.

---

[25]Sigmund Freud, *Introductory Lectures on Psychoanalysis*, trans. and ed. James Strachey (New York: Norton, 1966), p. 277.

[26]Ibid., p. 278.

Every person is, of course, unable to explicate some parts of his narrative, but in most cases this only causes local unintelligibility around certain issues. There are, however, some cases where a person is unable to explicate particularly important and wide-reaching parts of her narrative, or loses access to large parts of her life story. These situations have more extreme implications. A person with dramatic failures of articulation may be unable to comprehend a large proportion of his actions and emotions; a good part of what he says and does has the automatic character suggested by Freud's analogy with hypnosis; his personality is fragmented and fails to coalesce into a well-defined character; and he is impelled by forces he does not understand rather than behaving as an autonomous subject. In these cases, failure to meet the articulation constraint interferes with personhood as a whole.

In Chapter 6 I offer an extended discussion of the relation between consciousness and moral responsibility, self-interested concern, compensation, and survival, filling out the argument that the sense in which those elements of our narratives which we cannot articulate are less our own than those that we can is the one most relevant to our present pursuits. The general idea, however, should be clear. The features of our narratives that are below the surface *are* revealing of who we are, because they represent the missing elements of our explicit life stories—they fill in the pieces that make the incomprehensible elements of our explicit stories intelligible. In essence, then, they tell us what aspects must be incorporated into an explicit narrative for a given person to develop fully as a person. Nonetheless, until and unless they are seen and acknowledged by the subject herself, they play a different sort of role in her life than articulated aspects of her narrative, and so are less fully hers. They are, therefore, less attributable to her in the sense that is relevant to the four features, and so less fully hers in the sense that the narrative self-constitution view is trying to capture.

The Reality Constraint

In addition to the articulation constraint, the narrative self-constitution view requires that an identity-constituting self-narrative fundamentally cohere with reality. The motivation for this constraint should be clear. To be a person in the sense at issue here is to be able to engage in certain kinds of activities and interactions with others, and living the life of a person requires living in the same world as other persons. Fundamental agreement on the most basic features of reality is required for the kinds of interactions that take place between persons to be possible. A narrative that reveals the narrator to be deeply out of touch with reality is thus undermining of personhood and hence cannot—at least with respect to those elements of the narrative which seem grossly inaccurate—be identity-constituting.

There are, however, two observations that must be made about this constraint right away. First of all, the facts with which an identity-constituting narrative must cohere obviously cannot be facts about persons *per se*, or the narrative self-constitution view would be viciously circular. On this view the kinds of facts to which a narrative must be responsible are thus not facts about persons, but facts about human beings and their environments. The question of which *person* did what is to be settled by the narrative self-constitution view. The question of which *human body* did what is, however, one that can be settled by direct observation, photographs, videotapes, fingerprints, DNA samples, and similar evidence. It must be acknowledged, of course, that there is a complex and intimate connection between sameness of human body and sameness of person. Indeed, this connection is so close that at points in the discussion that follows it may look as if I am failing to distinguish between the two. Despite this appearance, I actually maintain the distinction between persons and human beings, and in the next section I explore and clarify the intricacies of the relation the narrative self-constitution view sees between the two.

The second point that must be made clear about the reality constraint is that it cannot be taken as an absolute demand. The narratives of most persons contain mistakes about even simple, directly observable facts—facts about which human beings were present on which occasions, or about the order in which events occurred, or about which voice made what utterance. The demand that in order to constitute himself as a person an individual needs to construct a self-narrative that is *completely* accurate is obviously far too severe. In order to incorporate the reality constraint, then, the narrative self-constitution view must provide guidelines about which kinds of errors are identity-compromising and which are not, as well as specifying exactly what is to be said about identity in those cases where errors do occur.

The facts with which the reality constraint requires coherence can be split into two basic categories, roughly these may be called basic observational facts and interpretative facts. The former category involves information taken in immediately through the senses, and the latter conclusions about the meanings or implications of those facts. To better understand the demands of the reality constraint I look at some examples in each category and discuss the judgments of the narrative self-constitution view in each case. A general picture of what this constraint involves should emerge.

ERRORS OF FACT

To begin with the most extreme kind of case, consider dramatic errors about basic, well-established, matters of observable fact. I have in mind here the kinds of errors in narrative that make the narrator seem clearly insane and deeply out of touch with reality. The narrative self-constitution view holds that such errors undermine the particular claims of self-attribution associated with the errors and also diminish the overall degree of personhood of the narrator. The kinds of delusional self-conceptions often urged as counterexamples against self-constitution views provide examples of this kind of narrative error. Take, for instance, the case of someone who believes himself to be Napoleon, insists that he led the troops at the Battle of Waterloo, and experiences deep shame and remorse about the outcome of that battle. Such a person might be said to have a self-narrative that includes Napoleon's actions at Waterloo, but we certainly cannot endorse a view of identity that attributes these actions to him. The narrative self-constitution view is saved from this unwelcome implication by the reality constraint. A few moment's reflection on the nature of such delusions shows that they can be rejected on the grounds that they force obvious and easily detectable errors about the narrator's immediately observable environment.

To see this, simply imagine the broader psychological context in which a Napoleonic delusion might reside. Imagine, for instance, pressing the alleged Napoleon by asking him questions of the following sort: What year do you think it is now? How many years ago does that make the Battle of Waterloo? Were you in the same body then that you are now? How long do you think human bodies typically last? Do you think yours is exceptional? How tall do you think you are? Do you recognize the body in this wedding photo as your own? Do you remember getting married? Do you think this woman is Josephine? And so on. Such questions, one assumes, will reveal one or another major anomaly in the individual's self-narrative. The claim to be Napoleon will, with pressure, fall apart. The individual claiming to be Napoleon will need to deny facts about what year it is, what objects are around him, what happens to human bodies over time, or the physical characteristics of the body making the claim—indeed his narrative will be inaccurate on not just one but several of these fundamental facts. These kinds of mistakes—being wrong by over 150 years about the current date, denying the most basic truths about human bodies (they do not live for much over 100 years; they do not usually grow 5 inches in adulthood, or transform radically in appearance, and so on)—are precisely the kind that make us at once recognize a deep pathology, and the reality constraint allows the claim to Napoleon's actions to be rejected because it is the source of those errors.

Moreover, it should be clear that the inclusion of wildly false claims such as those which must be involved in the narrative of the Napoleonic madman decreases the overall degree of personhood of the individual making the claims. The failure to be tuned into basic facts about the world one inhabits—and hence the failure to inhabit a world in common with one's fellows—interferes with the capacities and activities that define the lives of persons. This can be seen in practice. We do not hold psychotics responsible for their actions in the same way we do ordinary persons; we do not generally deem them capable of tending to their own affairs or looking after their own interests. Indeed, the contemplation of descent into a complete and vicious madness may well be anticipated as a sort of terrible personal death—a loss of self to a horrible intruder.

The situation is complicated, however, by the fact that psychosis is rarely so all-consuming. Even those with delusions of being Christ or Napoleon often show a great deal of contact with reality in the rest of their narratives and are able to interact and conduct themselves as persons in a number of contexts. Such people may be able to provide, for instance, a basically accurate account of what they have done for the last few weeks, or to take care of some of their treasured personal belongings, or to maintain rich and rewarding relationships with family members or friends. The autonomy, capacities, and activities associated with personhood are generally not eliminated by psychological illness of this type, but diminished, and so is the degree of personhood assigned by the narrative self-constitution view. It is important to emphasize once again that the narrative self-constitution view does not judge a narrative to be deficient in this way because it contains mistakes about a person's identity, but rather because it contains mistakes about clear and obvious facts about the world.

The reality constraint thus provides an easy way to reject self-narratives that contain a clearly inaccurate view of the world, because such narratives fail to appreciate obvious, observable facts. Not all inaccuracies in self-narrative are so dramatic, however. The narrative of every person is likely to contain a number of trivial errors—distortions and misrememberings that certainly do not indicate insanity or a lack of personhood. Someone may remember making a witty remark during a seminar when it was really her colleague;[27] or be convinced that she has never seen the person currently

---

[27]By "really her colleague who made the remark" I mean that the words came out of the body identified with her colleague—just as "remembering she made the remark" means that

being introduced to her although she has met him before and simply forgotten; or insist that the grocery store in her old neighborhood was on Eighty-
fifth street when it was really on Eighty-seventh. We take it as a matter of
course that such mistakes are part of life. Saying that their presence in
someone's narrative prevents her from constituting herself as a person is
obviously too extreme.

To see what the narrative self-constitution view can say about such errors, it is worth pointing to some major ways in which narrative inaccuracies of this sort differ from the more dramatic errors described above. First,
they are not recalcitrant in the same way. The person who makes such
mistakes in his self-narrative quickly retracts them when confronted with
evidence of his error. A tape recording of the colleague making the witty
remark leads to a correction of the claim that one made it oneself; a photograph of oneself (or at least one's body) with the person one does not
remember leads to the recognition that one *has* after all met him; and an old
telephone book showing the grocery to have been on Eighty-seventh Street
will alter the narrator's conception of where she used to shop.

Even more important than the typical willingness of people to revise their
narratives when presented with evidence of these small errors, is their ability
to do so easily. This points to a second major difference between extreme
and minor errors. In the case of minor errors the events described in the
narrative, though not accurate to the facts, are the kind of thing that might
easily have been true—it does not strain credulity to believe that things
might really have been as the people in our examples erroneously believe
them to be. The stories they are telling (unlike those we discussed earlier
containing extreme errors) are credible—even though they contain inaccuracies. Narratives containing minor factual errors thus cohere with the basic
contours of reality even though they do not match it in every particular.

Saying that the stories these people tell might really have happened
amounts to noticing that the errors they make do not, in the end, have many
implications. Things would not be much different if the person appropriat-
ing the witty remark really *had* made it, or if the grocery store really *had*
been two blocks over. In fact, many of these trivial errors are made concerning events only dimly remembered and the inaccurate details play only a
very minor role in the person's evolving narrative. The witty remark that the
person misremembers uttering in the seminar probably enters into her

---

she remembers it as being made by the human being making the memory claim. At first this
may seem to equate persons with human beings, but in fact does not—as we see in the next
section, "Personal Identity and Human Identity."

narrative only by reinforcing a general sense of herself as a funny person—providing a feeling of confidence around her colleagues, or an increased tendency to make jokes. For these purposes it matters very little whether she actually made *this* remark or some other one, so long as making a witty remark in a seminar would not be anomalous for her.

On reflection, it seems clear that a majority of the features of our life narratives are like this—their most important role comes from the general features or attributes they reflect rather than the actual details of the event. Indeed, there is some question exactly what the memory consists in, and what gets appropriated into the narrative. Individual human beings—who serve as our paradigmatic sources of personhood—are subjected to an incredible number of stimuli and have an enormous number of experiences. A person emerges when such an individual does the psychological work required to organize this experience in an ongoing, self-reflexive narrative. It is obviously impossible that this narrative should contain each and every event befalling the human being in full detail—such a goal would result in a Proustian paralysis in which the recognizable general features required for a coherent story would be lost in the richness of information.

There is a strong movement in contemporary psychology to look at memory not as a *reproductive* but rather a *reconstructive* process. Autobiographical memory, according to this view, is not arranged primarily to store specific information about the past, but to summarize, condense, and generalize our histories in a way that captures the important information about both ourselves and our pasts that those histories yield. A memory of making a witty remark may serve, that is, as an emblem of one's wittiness and of the kinds of interactions one generally has with colleagues. A memory of a lonely dinner in a new house may serve to recall all of the loneliness and insecurity associated with moving to a new town. A blur of memories of a variety of different outings and social events may generally represent a particularly fun and exciting time in a person's life. What is important for these memories is that they accurately represent general features about the person and his history, not necessarily that they are faithful to the facts.

It is on the basis of this kind of analysis, as well as several empirical studies that Craig Barclay and Peggy DeCooke conclude that "autobiographical recollections are not necessarily accurate, nor should they be; they are, however, mostly congruent with one's self-knowledge, life themes, or sense of self."[28] They say further that,

[28]Craig R. Barclay and Peggy A. DeCooke, "Ordinary Everyday Memories: Some of the Things of Which Selves Are Made," in Ulric Neisser and Eugene Winograd, eds., *Remembering Reconsidered: Ecological and Traditional Approaches to the Study of Memory* (Cambridge: Cambridge University Press, 1988), p. 92.

As with allegory, autobiographical memory often is a *constructive* and *reconstructive* process used to condense everyday memories of events and activities, extracting those features that embrace and maintain meaning in one's self-knowledge system. In turn, seemingly unconnected episodic recollections become allegorical in that particular events can be remembered and used as instances of generalized life experiences to convey one's sense of self to an audience.[29]

If our autobiographical memories are the way we tell ourselves and others the story of our lives, a consideration of the way these memories really work suggests that we are rather subtle authors. We do not need to resort to crude, literal reproduction of our physical and psychological histories, but can pick and choose the important elements, use sophisticated representational devices, and shape a story that can express what we take to be the basic and essential information about our lives.

This is important, because it suggests that there are two kinds of error or inaccuracy that can be present in a person's autobiographical narrative. An element of a narrative can be inaccurate to bald, observational facts about the world and yet accurate in terms of the general themes and information it conveys, or it can be inaccurate even to these. This analysis helps to show what the narrative self-constitution view can say about these less extreme errors. First, insofar as they represent detailed and specific claims about actions undertaken by a person with a certain body at a certain time, they are ruled out by the reality constraint. If a person's narrative contains a specific recollection of making someone else's witty remark, then the fact that that remark came from a different mouth than the one remembered (a fact in principle discoverable by tapes or eyewitness testimony) means that that specific claim should not be taken to be identity-constituting. However, insofar as the recollection expresses a general view of the person that does not conflict with any facts, that general self-ascription (I am a witty person; I have congenial relations with my colleagues) does not violate the reality constraint and can be taken as part of an identity-constituting narrative. Finally, insofar as an individual's narrative is generally accurate to the facts, minor inaccuracies should not be taken to decrease the level of personhood as the gross inaccuracies of the man who thought he was Napoleon did.

INTERPRETIVE INACCURACIES

Sometimes even self-narratives that are basically accurate to observable facts about the world and about human bodies can seem clearly in error

---

[29]Ibid., p. 92.

because of their bizarre interpretation of those facts.[30] Here, too, the reality constraint can be brought into play, and here too there is a distinction to be drawn between interpretive claims that are outrageous and those which are, at least, somewhere within the realm of comprehension. Once again, I begin with the more extreme case.

Consider, for example, a paranoiac—someone who constantly sees in clearly innocent actions and gestures evidence of a sinister conspiracy directed against her. Such a person might reveal her paranoia with statements of the following sort: "Don't you see the way those people looked at me? They were trying to let me know that they're watching me and could kill me at any time." Or, "Do you see those people taking notes? They are keeping records of my movements which will be put in a file downtown." Or, "I think it's very interesting that everywhere I go I see people wearing blue suits, certainly that's no coincidence. The CIA is after me again." Assuming that the individual in question suffers no hallucinations (as paranoiacs sometimes do), her narrative contains no obvious errors about observable facts—presumably people are looking over at her, or taking notes, or wearing blue suits. The conclusions she draws from those facts seem so absurdly unwarranted, however, that we can easily recognize that the part of her narrative which involves the persecution is mistaken.

The reality constraint should be taken to cover these sorts of cases, as well as cases of error about observable facts. When someone draws grossly unsupportable inferences from observation, we have good reason to believe that the claims he is making are erroneous. Certainly being paranoid does *not* mean that they aren't out to get you, but the clear lack of justification for the perception of persecution *together with the fact that the individual himself believes this conclusion to be justified by the available evidence*, gives us grounds to reject these claims as errors of reason, if not errors of fact. Someone who believes that seeing a number of people in blue suits is evidence that the CIA is following her is simply not in touch with reality. The reality constraint thus holds that in cases like this, as in cases of gross factual error, the narrative self-constitution view does not take the alleged persecution to be part of the person's history, despite the role it plays in her narrative.

This kind of case is also like that of gross factual error in that the outlandish nature of the claims that are part of the paranoid's narrative not only discredit the claims themselves, but also diminish the overall degree of personhood. It should be obvious that the individual who sees the world in

---

[30]I thank Christopher Hoyt for emphasizing this point to me.

this way is going to have a much harder time interacting with others and engaging in the activities that are part of the life of a person than someone who has a more ordinary conception of the world. Seeing the facts as having implications wildly different from those others see makes taking one's place in the world of persons virtually impossible. The full life of a person is unavailable to those who make errors of interpretation of this sort, and so their degree of personhood is vastly decreased.

Things are, of course, complicated by the tendency here, as in the case of the man who thought he was Napoleon, for the kinds of errors that are destructive of personhood, though extreme, to be more local than they at first appear. A person with paranoid delusions may, for quite a while, be able to hold down a job, keep a marriage going, parent children, and do many of the other sorts of things that persons do. Paranoia will almost certainly interfere with these aspects of life, but it will not disrupt them entirely. This is because even a paranoid narrative will likely overlap with fundamental narrative form in enough ways that some integration into the realm of the personal is possible even for the greatly disturbed. The narrative self-constitution view does not force us to conclude that psychotics are not persons—rather it allows us to dismiss the elements of psychotic's narratives that are out of touch with reality, and to recognize that their delusions interfere with personhood and diminish it.

Of course the way that the discussion has been divided is an oversimplification in some respects. Errors of fact and interpretation are not, in general, hermetically sealed from one another, and the line between observation and interpretation is notoriously difficult to draw. Moreover, narratives that violate the reality constraint in one respect are also likely to violate it in another—paranoiacs, for instance, are especially prone to delusions of grandeur. I do not mean to imply, therefore, that the distinction between types of error I am making here is something that itself carries a great deal of weight.

What is particularly interesting about errors of interpretation, however, is how the extreme errors shade into minor ones. It is easy to find virtual consensus that the paranoid's judgments of persecution are unwarranted and express a break from reality, but everyday life reveals a number of harder cases. Everyone knows someone who, although not delusional, seems to have a warped view of the world—someone who believes he is always being discriminated against, or treated unsympathetically, or being taken advantage of, although he seems perfectly well-treated. There are many variations on this phenomenon—people who believe, with what seems from our perspective little reason, that everyone is making sexual advances toward them, or the depressed person who views life's ordinary vicissitudes as insurmountable barriers. In individual cases it is tempting to consider people with this kind of skewed view as being in some sense out of touch with reality—yet the case is much hazier than that of the diagnosable paranoiac.

Most notably, in these less extreme cases one has a great deal less confidence that one's own interpretation of the facts is the correct one. Perhaps the person claiming constant discrimination is tuned into a reality to which most of us are insensitive; although the person who perceives all interactions as sexual advances may look absurd, it does not seem impossible that Freud was right and there is some sort of sexual subtext to most encounters; and empirical work suggests that far from the depressed having an unrealistically pessimistic view of the world, the healthy have an unrealistically optimistic one. In cases where so-called errors of interpretation are relatively minor, it is far from obvious whose perception is really incorrect.

The depressed person, the suspicious person, the optimistic person, and the angry person might tell quite different narratives of the same events, but they are all comprehensible and in most cases it seems misguided to argue about which is the most accurate. For certain practical purposes (such as within the context of a discrimination suit) it is, of course, necessary to settle in favor of one narrative over another, but the difficulty and discomfort we usually feel in doing so only shows our willingness to grant legitimacy to a variety of perspectives. It is, of course, more problematic for those who perceive the world differently to interact with one another than for those who perceive the world in much the same way, but for the most part these problems do not undermine interaction altogether.

The narrative self-constitution view does not, therefore, take what might from some perspectives be considered errors of interpretation to be a threat to a narrative's identity-constituting powers. On the contrary, the possibility of these differences in style shows the link between identity as defined by the narrative self-constitution view and the concept of identity operative in discussions of identity crises. The perspective according to which a particular narrative interprets a series of commonly agreed-upon events is what gives it its individual style. The angry person is an angry person because her narrative is constructed through the lens of an angry eye—whereas the good-hearted person is good-hearted because his narrative and consequent actions flow from a good-hearted view. As long as a person's narrative is comprehensible and responsible to the basic facts it is not taken to violate the reality constraint, even if some of its logic may seem offbeat.

There is, however, one complication concerning this analysis that needs to be discussed. Depending on one's psychological views, one might hold that the somewhat skewed interpretations of events I have just described as differences in narrative style are in fact the result of a person's failure to make some part of her narrative explicit. For instance, the angry person may have an angry interpretation of all events because of an unacknowledged anger for her father; or the person constantly perceiving sexual advances may do so because of a repressed feeling of rejection and need for validation. If this is the case, then my earlier claim that these repressed events interfere with the identity-constituting characteristics of a narrative seems in tension with my claim here that they do not.

This is a difficult tension to resolve because individual cases vary so much, and because where one comes down on particular controversies in psychology plays so much of a role in determining how to think about these cases. Even so, it seems possible to distinguish in general between cases where some particular, unacknowledged event or emotion brings about elements that do not fit into the narrative of which they are part on the one hand—for example, the hostile brother's actions—and cases .where a person's overall personality and outlook are influenced by past events and emotions on the other. The hostile brother of my earlier example recognizes the actions he takes as actions that could generally be considered hostile— he would see them as hostile coming from someone else—and yet he refuses to recognize them as such in himself. This kind of internal inconsistency within a narrative (which can also be found in many cases of common self-deception) is different from the kind of overall interpretive stance I have been talking about in this discussion of narrative inaccuracy. There are, then, some cases where unacknowledged influences direct a person's narrative in ways that make it internally troubled and divided, and these interfere with personhood and identity in the ways described in the discussion of the articulation criterion. Yet there are also cases where acknowledged influences shape a general outlook (for example, the angry person may feel quite consciously mistreated by her parents as well as by the world), and there, I think it is fair to say, these influences are identity-shaping rather than identity-destroying.

Once again, however, these issues are difficult because so often different elements are intermixed in a particular narrative, and their interactions become very complex. Significant life events, articulated or not, can in some respects contribute to the shaping of identity while in particular instances interfering with the construction of an identity-constituting narrative. To know what to say about identity in any particular case would require too many details to include in the kind of brief sketch that can be given here.

Still as a general rule it can be said that insofar as the origins of a person's perspective and the influence it has on his narrative can be articulated, the narrative is constitutive of identity. When the origins of affect and their present influence cannot be articulated, however, elements of the narrative are likely to be incomprehensible and immune from self-conscious control, and those aspects of the narrative fail to be identity-constituting.

This discussion should have provided a good overall picture of the reality constraint and how it interacts with the articulation constraint. Together, these two constraints represent the major demands on an identity-constituting narrative. Before offering a general summary of the narrative self-constitution view, however, there is one more topic to address, and that is the connection this view implies between personal identity and human identity.

Personal Identity and Human Identity

One of the most fundamental questions raised in philosophical discussions of personal identity is whether a single person can inhabit more than one body—or perhaps exist with no body at all. This question finds expression in the contemporary literature in the dispute between those who believe that persons are to be identified with particular human beings and those who believe that personal identity in some sense transcends human identity— that is, between bodily continuity theorists and psychological continuity theorists. So far, I have emphasized the narrative self-constitution view's promise as a means of capturing the intuitions inspiring the psychological continuity theory. Now, with a more detailed account of this view on the table, we can see that it speaks to the intuitions behind bodily continuity theories as well. This is because the narrative self-constitution view recognizes an intimate connection between personal and human identity without equating the two.

To see this, we should begin by reviewing some of the motivations behind the bodily continuity theorists' identification of particular persons with particular human beings, as well as the counterintuitions offered by psychological continuity theorists. Bodily continuity theorists argue that persons just are human beings because the actions and experiences we wish to attribute to persons are, always, actions and experiences of human beings. Even when we allow that other kinds of animals might be persons, we still envision the actions and experiences of a person as belonging to a particular living organism. More important still, we do reidentify persons by reidentifying human bodies.

The extent to which persons are identified with particular bodies can be clearly seen by reconsidering the examples I used earlier in the discussion of narrative errors concerning matters of observable fact. Outside the context of a philosophical discussion it would pass without comment if someone said that she could see with her own eyes that the *person* claiming to be Napoleon was wrong, or that a videotape showed that the *person* who claimed to have made a certain witty remark was not the one who in fact did so. These kinds of claims imply that facts about personal identity are directly observable, and it is obvious that the relevant observations are observations of human beings (the man claiming to be Napoleon is far too young to be Napoleon; the man claiming to have made the witty remark does not look or sound like the man making it on the videotape). The move from discovering that a particular human being took some action to discovering that a particular person did is so close that it seems almost like no move at all.

It is against this backdrop that psychological continuity theorists offer their hypothetical puzzle cases to demonstrate that although they usually *do* not, personal and human identity *can* come apart. These theorists acknowledge that in general a person is associated with one and only one human body, but offer cases like body swaps and teletransportation to show that we can *imagine* situations in which a single person can inhabit more than one body. I have already acknowledged the depth of appeal of the intuitions elicited by these cases—something does seem very right about the claim that a person's identity is somehow detachable from that person's body. At the same time, however, we should not forget the undeniable intuitive pull toward a bodily criterion.

In my estimation, neither bodily continuity theorists nor psychological continuity theorists give enough credit to the intuitions underlying the other view. Bodily continuity theorists categorically deny the possibility of a single person inhabiting more than one body, whereas psychological continuity theorists seem to suppose that it is just some sort of happy accident that persons and bodies are usually in one-to-one correspondence. The narrative self-constitution view can, however, speak to both sets of intuitions—it explains that persons are, in our experience, associated with only one body and holds that it is a deep conceptual fact that in general a person's history involves only one body, yet still allows that it is not impossible in particular cases for a single person to be associated with more than one human body. Let us consider what this means in more detail.

First, the narrative self-constitution view explains that persons and human beings are usually in one-to-one correspondnce through its general requirement that to be a person one must grasp the cultural conception of a person and apply it to oneself. It is indisputably part of our culture's conception that in general a single person is associated with one and only one human body throughout her history—this is precisely what the intuitions supporting the bodily continuity theory show. Virtually any self-narrative that involves attributing to oneself the actions and experiences of more than one body would fail the very first requirement of narrative form—the demand that a person's self-conception follow the logic of the story of a person's life. A life narrative that involved taking actions and having experiences in a variety of different bodies would quite likely verge on being incomprehensible and at the very least would almost certainly reveal that the narrator had failed to understand some of the most basic features of personhood.

Despite the strong connection between persons and human beings drawn by this requirement, however, the narrative self-constitution view does not completely rule out the possibility that a personal history could involve more than one body. If someone *did* tell a story involving more than one body in such a way that it indicated a grasp of the intimate connection that usually holds between persons and human beings, the narrative self-constitution view could allow it as an identity-constituting narrative and so allow that a single person had actions and experiences in more than one body. We have a good idea of what such a story would be like because we have seen several examples in the hypothetical cases offered by psychological continuity theorists. These cases never begin by simply asking us to imagine one person inhabiting more than one body—they always offer elaborate accounts of how this could happen. The purpose of these cases is precisely to offer a sane and comprehensible story of how personal identity and human identity could diverge—a story that does not violate our fundamental concept of personhood.

Of course we do not have teletransporters or brain transplant surgeries, and so any currently existing individual with a narrative involving more than one body is violating the reality constraint. Empirical developments may, moreover, show these technologies to be deeply impossible. Nonetheless, the intelligibility of the stories psychological continuity theorists tell shows that in circumstances where these or similar technologies did exist it would be possible for a person to take actions or have experiences in more than one body, and this undercuts the strict conceptual *identification* of personal identity with human identity that bodily continuity theorists endorse.

The narrative self-constitution view can thus accommodate the intuitions psychological continuity theorists uncover about the ways in which personal and human identity could diverge. It is important to realize, however, that the narrative self-constitution view does not go as far as the psychological continuity theory in driving a wedge between human and personal identity. Psychological continuity theorists, once they recognize that persons are not simply to be identified with human beings, seem to view the connection between a particular person and a particular human body as more or less accidental. We can take sameness of body as evidence of sameness of person, these theorists say, because in fact these two usually go together. They seem, however, to see no *necessity* that in general the history of a single person should involve the actions and experiences of only one human being—that is just the way things happen to be.

The narrative self-constitution view, on the other hand, draws a much closer connection between the identity of persons and the identity of human beings. Although this view does allow that in particular cases the history of a person could diverge from that of a human being, it is not obvious that it allows for the possibility of a general and widespread divorce between personal and human identity as the psychological continuity theory does. This is because of the emphasis the narrative self-constitution view places on the social and interactive nature of personhood and personal identity. The very concept of personhood involves a social dimension—to be a person is to be able to engage with others in particular ways.

It should be clear that the social organization in which persons exist requires that we be able to reidentify one another. Furthermore, it is not sufficient for the kinds of activities and interactions that make up the lives of persons that close intimates be able to recognize one another with careful questioning—it is necessary that in general persons be able to recognize the persons with whom they and others interact. We do this by reidentifying human beings. The considerations that underlie the narrative self-constitution view make it clear that we cannot assume that *every* action of a particular human being is attributable to the associated person, but in general, determining which body took a certain action or had a certain experience is—and must be—a reliable means of determining which person did.

If there were no generally trustworthy link between personal and human identity, it is not at all clear that it would be possible for the institutions that support personhood to continue. To see this, consider a twist on a common puzzle case used to support psychological continuity theories. The standard case involves a futuristic society in which technology has been developed to copy and replace human brains. In this world human beings regularly have their brains replaced with copies that retain all of the memories, beliefs, desires, and so on of the original brain, but correct for the wear and tear of aging. I suggest that we imagine that a means is found for replacing worn bodies as well, but that it is too difficult and costly to custom make each one. Instead, many copies of four or five prototype bodies are made, and the copies of individual brains are placed within them.

It is obvious that insofar as we can imagine such a world at all, we must imagine it as very different from our own. Those in it would be left without any quick and reliable means of determining who they were dealing with, and it would be incredibly difficult—if possible at all—to maintain the kinds of social organizations that define our own culture. Interactions between individuals would be much different from our interactions, and this difference would make a difference to the psychological organization—and hence the subjectivity—of the individuals in this imagined world. It would thus provide an example of the kind of situation discussed earlier in the chapter—a culture without persons as we know them.

The point of this exercise in science fiction is to show that the narrative self-constitution view includes an intimate relationship between personal identity and human identity. Because the reidentification of human bodies plays such an important role in our social interactions, the narrative self-constitution view demands that it play a central role in the constitution of persons and personal identity, even though this view does not simply *identify* persons with human beings. The emphasis on the social aspects of personhood in the narrative self-constitution view demands that an identity-constituting narrative be responsible to how we are reidentified by others. Since we do reidentify persons by reidentifying human beings, this view demands a close conceptual relation between personal identity and the identity of human beings as well. The narrative self-constitution view is thus able to speak to the intuitions behind the psychological continuity theory, while respecting the close connection between person and body emphasized by bodily continuity theorists.

Once understood in all of its detail, the narrative self-constitution view should sound a great deal more plausible than it did initially. On this view, a person exists in the convergence of subjective and objective features. An individual constitutes herself as a person by coming to organize her experience in a narrative self-conception of the appropriate form (something that individual human beings do as a result of being socialized into their culture). "Appropriate form" is not something determined arbitrarily, but rather something that comes out of the complex lifestyles and social interactions definitive of personhood. The kind of narrative required is one that makes this lifestyle and set of interactions possible, and this involves, among other things, the demand that a person draw the limits of himself at essentially the same place that others do.

The narrative self-constitution view does allow some leeway and variation in self-conception. There are a wide range of narrative styles that can be identity-constituting, as long as they stay within a range of options that allow the narrator to lead the life of a person. Moreover, our initial sense of the identity of a person can be challenged or expanded in individual cases by unusual narratives. Further complications arise because both personhood and individual attributions of actions and experiences admit of degrees. In general, however, the content and form of an identity-constituting narrative is limited by our conception of persons. This conception itself, however, is not sufficient to determine identity. Unless an individual applies that conception to herself, forming a self-conception that coheres with it, she possesses neither the capacities nor the subjectivity that make a person.

A person's identity, according to the narrative self-constitution view, is created by narrating and living a life that recognizes the general cultural conception of a person, the objective view of one's own life, and facts about the world. This view of identity, unlike the psychological continuity theory, is able to account for the intuitive connection we draw between personal identity and survival, moral responsibility, self-interested concern, and compensation.

6

Characterization and the Four Features

With a developed alternative to the psychological continuity theory in hand, we are now in a position to return to the question of the link between personal identity and survival, moral responsibility, self-interested concern, and compensation, and to see how our change of subject from the reidentification to the characterization question has made it possible to understand this connection. The basic argument turns on a reinterpretation of the notion of sameness of consciousness. The extreme claim, you recall, follows from the inability of psychological continuity theorists to develop a notion of sameness of consciousness over time which makes that relation deep enough to underlie the four features. This, I suggested, was because the perspective of the reidentification question forces those who address it to conceive of sameness of consciousness in terms of reidentification—asking whether the consciousness at t_2 is the same consciousness as that at t_1. The switch to the characterization question allows us to think of sameness of consciousness in a whole new light, however, by pointing us toward issues of attribution.

No one denies that there is a deep and important connection between psychical elements attributed to the same consciousness at a single time—it matters profoundly whether the six words of a sentence are all attributed to a single consciousness or each is attributed to one of six separate consciousnesses. I contend that the deep connection involved in synchronous co-consciousness can be extended to temporally remote elements. Collections of actions and experiences that occur at different times can be attributed to a single consciousness if they are all part of a single identity-constituting narrative. I contend further that sameness of consciousness understood in this way can provide a basis for the four features. I begin my defense of these claims by considering some of the most important connections between psychical elements that are part of the same consciousness at a single time. These same connections hold between temporally remote elements that are part of a single identity-constituting narrative. And the kind of unity of consciousness generated by the creation of such a narrative provides a basis for the four features.

Sameness of Consciousness at a Single Time

The first step toward seeing how the narrative self-constitution view can provide a basis for the four features is to better understand the connections involved in the strong co-consciousness generally acknowledged to exist at one time. What is of interest here is not the *cause* of this co-consciousness (for example, it would not help for present purposes to come up with an account of the neurological basis of this relation in humans), but rather its qualitative *nature* (that is, what we are implying when we say that various psychical elements are part of the same consciousness). A development and defense of a comprehensive view of unity of consciousness is obviously beyond the scope of this discussion, but it is possible to identify some of the most crucial elements and to highlight the features that are relevant for our purposes.

To begin with, it seems clear that at least part of what is involved in different psychical elements being part of the same consciousness is that they mutually influence and inform one another—that each contributes to an interpretive context within which the others are experienced. Thus, in the consciousness of a six-word sentence, each word is interpreted in light of the other five; in ordinary perceptual experience, visual, auditory, tactile, and olfactory input, as well as cognitive factors, cohere to produce a unified experience; and when a subject hears a chord, it is the relation between the notes which is heard, as well as the notes themselves.

This last point is important, because it shows the depth of the mutual influence in co-consciousness. Indeed, although it is of course possible to identify different elements as part of a particular conscious experience, it is essential to recognize that it is somewhat artificial to think of experience in this way. On hearing a chord, one can, with attention, discern each of the notes, but the experience of the chord is not the experience of the individual notes heard separately. Similarly, although it is possible to abstract the various aspects of the experience of looking at the sea from a ship's railing, the experience itself is not an experience of a sea image *and* wave sounds *and* salt smell *and* peacefulness—it is an experience of looking at the sea, which contains all of these elements.

William James remarks on the depth of this connection in *Psychology*. There, talking about our thoughts and feelings he says,

> Take a hundred of them, shuffle them and pack them as close together as you can (whatever that may mean); still each remains the same feeling it always was, shut up in its own skin, windowless, ignorant of what the other feelings are and mean. There would be a hundred-and-first feeling there, if, when a group or series of such feelings were set up, a consciousness *belonging to the group as such* would emerge, and this one hundred and first feeling would be a totally new fact.[1]

For distinct thoughts and feelings to inform one another they must be part of one and the same consciousness; and as soon as they become part of the same consciousness, they are no longer disparate elements but aspects of one, unified experience.

The kind of unity James describes can be cashed out in terms of the implications it has for both the phenomenology of experience and the capacities of the subject. It is worth saying a bit about each of these. The phenomenological changes occur because the mutual influence of the different elements that are part of a single consciousness act as a lens through which the others are experienced. When a single subject is conscious of a six-word sentence, it is not experienced as six words side-by-side, but rather as a whole sentence, and that means that the experience of each word in the sentence is qualitatively different from the experience of each word in isolation. Similarly, the sensory experience of a dramatic thunderstorm is qualitatively different in a consciousness that also includes a terror of storms, or a worry about friends traveling in the rain, than in one which includes a feeling of how warm and cozy it is by the fire—even if the details of the sensory inputs themselves are identical in the two cases. The various elements in a unified consciousness influence and inform one another to create a unified whole, and so the qualitative experience of each element is conditioned by the others. In addition to its implications for phenomenology, the claim that different elements are part of the same consciousness has implications for a subject's capacities. There are certain tasks or responses that require the interaction of more than one bit of information; and so when a subject is able to perform those tasks or offer the appropriate response, we can conclude that the same consciousness possesses all of the requisite information. A person conscious of the sentence "He got money from the bank" can, for instance, confidently disambiguate "bank" in a way that a subject conscious only of the word "bank" cannot.

Provisionally, then, we can say that distinguishable but synchronous

---

[1]William James, *Psychology* (Cleveland: The Living Library, 1948), pp. 198–99.

psychical elements are part of the same consciousness if they mutually interact in a way that produces a unified experience in which each plays a role, and plays the role it does because it serves as an interpretive context for the others, which in turn provide its context. But this is not yet enough to capture what is uniquely characteristic of the relation of co-consciousness. We have already seen that elements that are not part of consciousness can also play a role in determining the nature of a subject's experience. Chapter 5's discussion of implicit narrative elements—especially the example of the man with unacknowledged hostility for his brother—made it abundantly clear that unconscious elements as well as conscious ones can affect experience. The Freudian examples emphasize the impact unconscious psychical elements can have on subjectivity. Examples of the effect they can have on capacities are found in a number of phenomena uncovered by work in contemporary psychology. Perhaps the kind of case most frequently discussed by philosophers in this regard is "blindsight," a situation in which patients who deny being able to see stimuli in certain parts of their visual field nevertheless demonstrate the capacity to act on the information provided by those stimuli. Despite their categorical insistence that they have no visual experience of a given stimulus, when asked to guess which of several presented alternatives represents the stimulus presented to them, these patients often perform almost without error.

Since even elements that are not part of consciousness can affect a subject's phenomenology and capacities, this influence alone is not enough to define co-consciousness. To assemble a useful definition of this concept, we must first distinguish between the kind of influence exerted on a person's psychological life by unconscious elements and that exerted by conscious elements. The means to make this distinction can be found in Chapter 5's discussion of the articulation constraint. There I argue that implicit elements of a person's narrative are only partially hers because their influence is more limited than that of elements that can be articulated. The impact on conscious experience and action of elements that cannot be articulated is more rigid and stereotyped than that of conscious elements, as Freud's analogy with posthypnotic suggestion implies. The kind of rigidity and automaticity of influence Freud identifies in neurotic symptoms is also noted by cognitive psychologists and neuroscientists discussing phenomena like blindsight.

Ran Lahav considers a number of cases of what is "often termed . . . in the neuropsychological literature, *implicit knowledge* . . . information whose existence in the brain is expressed through the subject's behavior, but the subject is not—what in ordinary language is called—'conscious' of having that information."[2] Some contemporary philosophers of mind (notably Kathleen Wilkes, Patricia and Paul Churchland, and Thomas Nagel) have argued that these phenomena show the concept of consciousness to lack scientific respectability. Their argument, roughly, is that any meaningful distinction between an element's being conscious and its being unconscious is undermined by the ability of those phenomena we call unconscious to affect behavior just as conscious phenomena do. Lahav takes on this objection, arguing that although cases of implicit knowledge do show that unconscious elements can affect external behavior "the effects of implicit and explicit knowledge on the subject's behavior are profoundly different."[3]

After a painstaking discussion of each of several kinds of implicit knowledge—blindsight, blind touch, agnosia, neglect, and the implicit knowledge that occurs in normal subjects—Lahav summarizes the difference he uncovers as follows:

> These considerations point to a compelling conclusion: Information of the type that is commonly described as conscious or explicit (and recall that the latter is commonly defined in terms of the former) has a profoundly different role in the cognitive system from information commonly described as nonconscious or implicit. Conscious experience expresses information available for an entire spectrum of global, integrated, and flexible (non-automatic) behaviors. It is therefore reasonable to make the hypothesis . . . that it constitutes a central *junction of information*, one in which information from different sources and modalities are integrated to produce a unified and coherent body of behaviors.
>
> In contrast, a piece of nonconscious (implicit) information is largely segregated from other information-processing events in the organism, and is therefore limited to exerting specific, isolated, or rigid effects on the cognitive system and on behavior.[4]

As in the case of the repression discussed by Freud, the nonconscious perceptions in blindsight exert a routinized or automatic influence.

Elements that are part of a person's psyche but not part of her consciousness can alter affect and behavior—sometimes profoundly—but they assert themselves, as it were, blindly. Their impact is not sensitive to context and cannot be modified to meet new circumstances or take account of new information. Although nonconscious psychical elements influence conscious life, they are not themselves directly influenced in return. They can-

---

[2] Ran Lahav, "What Neuropsychology Tells Us about Consciousness," *Philosophy of Science* 60, no. 1 (March 1993): 70.
[3] Ibid.
[4] Ibid., p. 79.

not be scrutinized in the light of what is known, and so cannot be revised, reconsidered, or reshaped in the light of the rest of the person's psychological life.[5] Nonconscious elements are thus not integrated into experience in the same way that conscious elements are.

We have, of course, no uncontroversial view of either consciousness or synchronous co-consciousness, and neither Freud nor Lahav can, alas, serve as a final authority. They do, however, converge on a highly plausible view in which an element is part of a subject's consciousness if it exerts an influence on her subjectivity and behavior that is flexible, global, and responsive, whereas elements that are unconscious exert an influence that is rigid, automatic, and stereotyped. Before seeing how this view of consciousness can provide a basis for the four features, it is important to note that flexibility and responsiveness are not all-or-nothing attributes—the influence of a psychical element on conscious experience and behavior can enjoy these characteristics to a greater or lesser extent. This of course implies that an element's being part of a subject's consciousness is also a matter of degree.

This should not be a difficult consequence to accept. Although there may be an initial impulse to think of consciousness as an all-or-nothing attribute, a bit of introspection makes it clear that a somewhat continuous line of demarcation between the conscious and unconscious more closely mirrors the phenomenology of consciousness. At any given time some elements are at the forefront of consciousness—the center of attention—and are having the most powerful influence on the overall character of experience. Other aspects are at the periphery—there and accessible, but pushed to the corner; others are not conscious but can easily be brought to consciousness; others cannot be made conscious without immense effort; and some may never come to consciousness at all. The view that consciousness

---

[5] I should make it clear that this does not mean that unconscious influences are entirely static—they can be quite malleable. As the outward circumstances and internal dynamics of a person's life change, unconscious material may adapt its mode of expression. It is, for instance, a commonplace that clearing up a psychological symptom without getting to the unconscious material that causes it is more likely to create a new symptom than it is to cure the patient. Thwarted in its previous mode of expression, the unconscious material finds an alternative route to the world. What is in the unconscious may thus have a fairly wide repertoire in terms of the affect and action to which it leads. My claim that unconscious material is rigid should not, therefore, be taken to indicate that there is only one effect it can have, but rather that it cannot be directly affected by what is part of consciousness, and so cannot be integrated into a coherent whole. Whatever form of expression unconscious material takes, it is incomprehensible to the person in whom it occcurs, and he is thus not able to evaluate and mitigate these effects easily through conscious reflection. I thank Mark Jenkins for pointing out the importance of clarifying this issue.

is not a univocal state is increasingly less controversial and has the support of psychologists and philosophers of mind alike.

Sameness of Consciousness over Time

The primary defining feature of synchronous co-consciousness—that co-conscious elements influence one another in a way that brings about changes in subjectivity and capacities—can apply to psychical features that are spread out over time as well. Indeed, on the narrative self-constitution view this kind of influence is exactly what is required for actions and experiences to be part of the same identity-constituting narrative. As we saw in Chapter 5, creating an autobiographical narrative is not simply composing a story of one's life—it is organizing and processing one's experience in a way that presupposes an implicit understanding of oneself as an evolving protagonist. A large part of what that entails is that the remembered past and anticipated future exert an influence on the present—that they serve as its interpretive context, the lens through which it is experienced.

Chapter 5 also contained a number of examples of the ways in which the incorporation of actions and experiences into one's narrative alters subjectivity. The discussion of the impact in later life of youthful financial security or parental approval, as well as the extended description of *Now Voyager's* Charlotte Vale (see Chapter 5, pages 110–14), shows just how deeply past actions and experiences can influence the nature of present subjectivity, whereas the contrast between poverty as experienced by the graduate student and by the discouraged welfare father shows the difference forward-looking appropriation can make. It should also be obvious that a similar case can be made for a change in capacities. The capacity to interact with other people in certain ways, for instance, depends on having a history with them as part of one's narrative, or an expectation of an intersecting future.

At a glance, then, it certainly seems as if the relation of co-consciousness that can hold between psychical elements that occur at the same time can also hold between elements that occur at different times, and thus that a relation of sameness of consciousness just as deep and important as that which exists at one time can be extended over time. It is important to see that this analysis does not rely on *reidentifying* a consciousness at different times (whatever that would mean). Rather, it suggests that just as we recognize that there is a meaningful line to be drawn around the experiences that are part of a single consciousness at any given moment, so is there a meaningful line to be drawn around those experiences spread out over time that are part of a single consciousness—indeed, the former will be a subset of the latter.

We acknowledge that the depth of connection between psychical elements that are synchronously co-conscious is such that they are not properly thought of as a number of separate elements that are somehow all together in the same container—a "consciousness"—but rather as having interacted in such a way as to fuse into a unified whole that includes some version of each, modified by its context (recall the quotation from James given earlier). What the narrative self-constitution view suggests is that something similar happens for elements spread out over time that are part of the same narrative. The moments of conscious awareness in a single person's life are not distinct entities that are somehow strung together, but rather a dynamic interactive system that integrates to produce a subjectivity that extends over time.

The difference I am trying to point to can perhaps be seen more clearly by thinking about some of the metaphors that are often used in discussions of personal identity, as well as one of my own. A common way of describing the relation between the different temporal parts of a person's life as understood by a sameness of substance view (a view that personal identity consists in either sameness of body or of soul) is by analogy with beads on a sting. The string represents the continuing person, and the individual beads the person's distinct experiences, which are all his by virtue of being on the same string. Reductionists, on the other hand, use the metaphor of a river or stream to express the kind of unity persons have. Sameness of river does not, they point out, imply sameness of water, but rather continuity of flow. Similarly, reductionists claim, persons consist in the steady stream of different experiences.

In contrast to both of these conceptions, the narrative self-constitution view sees the composition of a person as more like that of a complicated soup or stew. A soup is, of course, made of different ingredients, and these must exist prior to the soup itself. Once they are mixed together, however, they interact to produce something that is not best understood as a mere collection of ingredients laid out in some particular arrangement. Each ingredient contributes to the flavor of the whole and is itself altered by being simmered together with the others. A soup can, of course, be divided into portions, but the character of each portion is determined by the soup from which it came.

In a like manner the experiences woven together into a person's narrative interact and alter one another in such a way that the narrative itself becomes the primary unit. The narrative is like the soup into which experiences are thrown, seasoning and altering one another—the past is reinterpreted and experienced in a new light in virtue of the present; the expectation of the future gives a different taste to current experience; and future experiences will have their character within the context of the whole. The experience of a person is thus had by an extended narrative subject, and not by a time-slice.

In this way the narrative self-constitution view provides a unity of con- sciousness over time that is just as deep, and has implications just as impor- tant, as unity of consciousness at any given time. Those who deny the possibility of any kind of real extension of consciousness over time—de- fenders of Parfit, for example—might argue that the kinds of connections I have described do not really signal a *deep* connection between distinct mo- ments of consciousness, they only show that in the daily course of events memories and anticipations are part of our psychological makeup and in- fluence the character of consciousness at any given time. It is, the argument would continue, the memories and anticipations, rather than the past and future themselves that have the impact I have described, and so conscious- ness must still be viewed as essentially punctual. Support for this view might take the form of a claim that at any given moment consciousness must have some quality, and that although that quality is *usually* determined by the person's past and future, it is at least in principle reproducible in someone who had not really had that past and will not have that future—in someone who would, in fact, exist for only an instant.

Of course I do not deny that there is a quality of consciousness at every moment, but I do question the assumption that even in principle that qual- ity could be reproduced in an instant, or outside the context in which it naturally occurs. I contend that scrutinizing a slice of consciousness re- moved from its ordinary context is exactly the wrong way to look at things. It does not illuminate but obscures the most interesting facts about persons and their distinctive subjectivity. Anything whole can (at least in imagina- tion) be sliced into bits—the question is what is gained or lost in doing so. It is by no means obvious that the most essential part of a person's experi- ence at any time can be reproduced in an independent time-slice, even if we imagine that slice containing all of the relevant forward- and backward-looking elements.

The point that I am making here is simply that the contribution the past and future make to the present is more than just the production of memo- ries and anticipations, it is something deeper. Wollheim expresses this quite clearly when he points out that there are *two* ways the recognition of oneself as temporally extended enters into the phenomenology of the present. He says,

> The phenomenology of past and future states is not just something that we infer to be the case. It inheres in the present. There are two ways in which it is continually brought home to us. One is through ourselves and what we are. For entering into present states, we do so as persisting creatures who will enter into future states and have entered into past states. The other way is through the mental states themselves and what they are like. For amongst present mental states are included memories of past states and what I shall . . . call pre-visagements of future states, which through their own phenomenology exhibit, rather than merely provide evidence for, the phenomenology of the states they represent.[6]

Here I am emphasizing the first, broader contribution that the past and future make to the present.

Think about being given a piece of a story—one event or episode—reproduced in all of its detail. It might well be obvious from the form and character of that episode that it is part of a larger story, and recognizing that already adds something to how we understand the bare elements presented. If we do not have the rest of the story, however, the piece we do have does not read as it would if we had come to it from the beginning of the story. This is because the earlier parts of the story provide information and engender certain expectations that still further enrich the understanding of the episode in question. It is not altogether obvious that the impact of this history can be reproduced in a moment. Certainly there is nothing one could add to the description of the episode—short of the story itself—which would do so. I suggest that our experience, too, has this character; it is essentially something that takes place over time, and whose relevant attributes cannot be caught in a moment, or even in a series of moments, if these are considered in principle separable from one another.

Matters of conceptual priority are, of course, difficult to argue for directly—it is often not even clear what counts as evidence in such disputes. A look at some of the different arrangements of psychological experience actually found in everyday life, however, greatly strengthens my claim that the organization of experience into a narrative self-conception actually changes the nature of subjectivity in a way that is reasonably described as the creation of a temporally extended experiencing subject who is conceptually prior to its experience. In the ordinary course of events we encounter

---

[6]Wollheim, *The Thread of Life*, p. 256.

a number of human beings who, for a variety of reasons, do not have narrative self-conceptions, and a comparison of their mental life with ours is deeply instructive.

There are, first of all, human infants. Newborns lack the cognitive apparatus necessary to conceive of themselves as distinct individuals persisting through time, and although there are a great many different theories about the precise nature of the process by which a developing child comes to distinguish itself from the rest of the world and perceive itself as continuing over the course of an intelligible life, there is no doubt that this is something that does happen. Infants do not narrate their lives, but take individual experiences as they come. In becoming socialized the developing child learns to live a certain kind of life, to think of persons—and hence of itself—in a certain way, thus *learning* to integrate experience into a coherent narrative whole.

This development of psychological organization is associated with profound phenomenological changes. The inner life of an infant may no longer be conceived as the whirring, buzzing confusion famously described by William James, but it seems quite obvious nonetheless that it is vastly different from the inner life of an adult. Precisely because the various moments of experience come to infants completely out of context—because they cannot be put into a schema or viewed as part of a larger unfolding of events through which the subject stays constant—the infant does not have the kind of subjective life that an ordinary adult human being has. It is reasonable, moreover, to view infantile consciousness as somewhat like the punctual or serial consciousness that psychological continuity theorists describe. The infant cannot project itself forward or backward—it is, at any moment, as if the past and future do not exist. Compared to the subjectivity experienced by adult human beings, infancy seems much more like a case where we can think of consciousness in terms of time-slices, each of which is a more or less independent psychological subject.[7] Notably, infants and very young children also do not have in their repertoire the kinds of psychological activities that require persistence through time and are definitive of persons.

Infancy is not the only example of consciousness without narrative capacity, however. This same dissolution into parts can be seen in certain pathologies. One of the most notorious examples is found in cases of severe

[7]Of course, even this is probably an exaggeration. Although infantile consciousness likely has a great many punctual aspects, it is most probable that even from birth there are a great many underlying integrative processes that create a rudimentary persisting subject—processes that may well be necessary for developing the more full-blown narrative capacities that are characteristic of persons.

dementia, such as that encountered in late-stage Alzheimer's patients. Those who suffer from this condition begin to lose the glue that holds their lives together. They no longer recognize persons important to them, lose touch with their pasts, are at a loss to understand how they came to be where they are, no longer know how to anticipate the implications of the present for the future, and so on. Those who suffer from dementia are robbed of precisely the ability to pull their lives together into a coherent story; they become terrified and confused because they cannot put the pieces together.

Once again, there is a great deal to be learned by considering the phenomenology of such cases. We believe that those who suffer from dementia undergo a marked change in subjectivity. In some sense we believe that their consciousness diminishes—when we imagine someone becoming more and more senile we imagine her sinking deeper and deeper into a twilight state of semiconsciousness. The consciousness and capacities of a person suffering this sort of confusion seem clearly less desirable than our own—the prospect of losing the kind of organization of experience we usually possess to dementia is, for most of us, horrifying and depressing. Added to these phenomenological changes, the loss of narrative powers clearly brings about a change in capacities. Individuals who cannot process their experiences as ordinary adult humans do and so lose the flow of their lives, find themselves unable to participate in many of the activities and practices that stand at the core of the lives of persons.

This loss of capacities, which is obvious in dementia, can perhaps be seen even more clearly in other kinds of traumatic brain disorders where additional kinds of physical decline do not obscure the issue. There are a number of well-known instances of individuals who, because of damage to the brain through disease, illness, or drug and alcohol abuse, have lost the ability to form long-term memories, and hence to construct a narrative of their lives. This inability has proved devastating. These people are unable to engage in close, intimate relationships with others. They cannot remember people they meet for more than a few minutes and see them as strangers over and over again. There is thus no possibility of building up a history with another person, learning from mistakes (or triumphs), developing skills, or evolving as a person.

A consideration of the phenomenology we imagine in these pathological cases offers an interesting contrast to the subjective life of ordinary adult humans. In dementia and the neural pathologies of memory, we see individuals with a consciousness that cannot be pulled together into a coherent whole. There are moments of conscious experience, but they remain cut off from those which went before and those which come after, and so each one comes and goes without connection to the past and future. We do not, however, think that this lack of influence between the different moments of consciousness is simply something noted from the outside. It is something that is also *experienced* from the inside. As in the case of infancy, we believe the independence of the different moments of conscious awareness in someone with one of these pathologies leads to a truly punctuated consciousness. These subjects' awareness is not spread out over time but consists in a series of disconnected episodes.

When we compare the subjectivity of infants or those suffering from profound dementia or memory-related neural disorders with that of healthy adult human beings, we can see an important sense in which the consciousness and subjectivity of the latter should be conceived to be spread out over time rather than made up of a series of independent time-slices. The phenomenological life of an individual who narrates her life in the way we narrate ours is much different from that of an individual who does not. The pulling together of events and experiences occurring at different times into a single narrative does more than simply change the quality of conscious experience at a given moment, it changes the quality of conscious experience overall—narrators have a consciousness that extends over time. A new psychological and behavioral repertoire comes into being when an individual forms an identity-constituting self-conception and is lost when the narrative thread is lost.

Of course there are, as always, complications with this analysis. Since having a narrative is a matter of degree, so are the changes in capacity and phenomenology I have been describing. A developing child does not create a narrative (and so an extended consciousness) all at once, nor does a victim of dementia lose narration in one devastating moment. As the interaction and integration of different temporal parts of a life becomes more intense, and involves increasingly distant events, the individual's phenomenological life becomes more and more like that of an adult human being, and more widely extended. As the connections get broken and the range of influential experiences narrows, similarity to the phenomenological life of a person diminishes. Real cases are, of course, messy. A person in late-stage Alzheimer's may be unable to retain anything in short-term memory, yet have vivid recollections of childhood friends. The important element in these cases, however, is the loss of narrative capacity, and even though such an individual may have memories of long ago, he cannot integrate these with anything else, or have any kind of coherent sense of himself as an extended subject. The effects on consciousness are dramatic, and the differences between his consciousness and ours profound.

The connection that holds between elements that are part of the same identity-constituting narrative and hence, according to the narrative self-constitution view, attributable to the same person, is thus parallel to the connection that holds between elements that are synchronously co-conscious. This makes the relation between events attributed to the same person by this view as deep and important as that between elements that are part of the same consciousness at a single time. The formation of an identity-constituting narrative alters the nature of an individual's experience in a way that extends consciousness over time, producing a persisting experiencer who is the primary experiencing subject. What remains to be shown is that the four features, which psychological continuity theorists have so much trouble accounting for, are appropriate to a subject of this kind.

Sameness of Consciousness and the Four Features

Most of the work necessary to show that the narrative self-constitution view can account for the link between personal identity and the four features has already been done. In Chapter 3 we saw that psychological continuity theories are inherently unable to capture the four features because they do not allow for the persistence of a single, experiencing subject, and such persistence is necessary to make sense of the attitudes and practices surrounding these features. Survival involves the continuation of the same experiencing subject; moral responsibility requires that the experiencing subject who commits a crime be the one to experience the punishment; self-interested concern requires that the person having an experience in the future be the one who anticipates it, and compensation demands that the same experiencing subject who suffers a sacrifice enjoy the later benefits. In order to capture the connection between personal identity and the four features, then, we need a view according to which personal identity implies sameness of experiencing subject.

We have seen that the narrative self-constitution view is just such an account. The formation of an identity-constituting narrative creates a single, temporally extended subject of experience, and any two actions or experiences attributed to the same person by this view are necessarily attributable to the same subject of experience. It is thus fairly clear, at least in general terms, that the narrative self-constitution view is able to avoid the extreme claim and to illuminate our intuitions concerning personal identity and the four features. This general claim can, however, be strengthened and clarified by considering the relation between identity as defined by the narrative self-constitution view and each of the four features in turn.

Consider first survival, which is in some ways the most basic of the four. It is also probably the feature hardest to link to the narrative self-constitution view. This is at least in part, as I have already noted, because we have many different notions of survival. Simple biological survival is an extremely important and basic concept for us, and a person's self-narrative obviously does not determine that. Nor, however, is biological survival the survival that psychological continuity theorists are trying to capture. Those theorists are tapping our intuitions about a notion of *personal* survival—the continuation of the *self*—which they believe can be distinguished from the continuation of the body.

In order to capture our intuitions about survival and identity, the narrative self-constitution view must thus demonstrate that the possession of the appropriate sort of self-conception is linked to personal survival. It must also show that this view makes sense of the importance survival has for us. As we saw in Part I, one of the chief complaints against the psychological continuity theory is that it cannot explain why we should care about survival as this view defines it. To demonstrate the viability of the narrative self-constitution view, then, we must show that the creation of a narrative self-conception constitutes a kind of survival that it makes sense to care about.

This can be done by attending to how the creation of a self-narrative brings about profound changes in an individual's phenomenology and abilities. Both the subjectivity and the capacities definitive of living the life of a person are, as I have already shown, tied directly to the possession of an identity-constituting narrative of the form defined in the narrative self-constitution view. Failure to create such a narrative entails the failure to become a person, and the loss of a narrative by an individual who has formed one constitutes that person's demise. This conclusion does not, moreover, rely on a mere technicality of definition. To see this we need only reconsider examples of humans who fail to have such narratives.

Although I allow that there may be many alternative ways of organizing experience (not all of which need be considered inferior to our own) the most common actual cases of human beings without narratives are the ones already discussed in this chapter—infants and sufferers from dementia. Certainly there is a real sense in which it is right to say that never to develop out of the psychological organization of infancy is never to exist as a person at all; and to contemplate a descent into a second infancy such as that present in late-stage Alzheimer's is, as has been observed repeatedly, to contemplate the loss of oneself—a personal death. In short, the formation of a narrative self-conception of the proper form creates a persisting subject with the phenomenological life and set of capacities peculiar to persons, and these last only as long as the narrative does. The elements in terms of which we define ourselves as persons stand and fall with the continuation of an autobiographical narrative, and so there is a clear link to be drawn between identity as defined by the narrative self-constitution view and personal survival.

What remains to be shown is that the narrative self-constitution view can explain the importance personal survival bears for us. Before undertaking this task, it is crucial to recognize that *explaining* the importance of survival could mean giving an account of why survival *is* important to us or it could mean justifying why survival *should* be important to us. The sense of explanation relevant here is the former, not the latter. Psychological continuity theorists start from the brute fact that identity bears a particular practical significance in our everyday lives. Part of this significance rests in the fact that identity is held to determine survival—for a person to survive is for that very person to continue to exist. It is thus taken as a prima facie constraint on a theory of identity that whatever relation is used to define identity should be one that matters to us in the way that survival does. What is required is thus to define identity in such a way that it makes sense of the fact that we *do* care about it as we do, not to show that it is *worth* caring about in some absolute sense.

The problem with the psychological continuity theory is that it fails to meet even this weaker requirement. The relation in terms of which it defines identity—and ultimately survival—is a relation that does not matter to us as survival does. Even taking the fundamental values of persons for granted, then, psychological continuity theorists cannot account for the simple fact that survival is important to us. The narrative self-constitution view, on the other hand, fares far better in this regard.

We have already seen that the narrative self-conception in terms of which this view defines identity has a great deal of practical significance. The loss of a self-narrative puts a stop to the kind of experience, actions and, interactions uniquely enjoyed by persons, and so the end of a self-narrative ends the experiencing subject and agent who was the person. An individual who has lost her narrative is no longer able to lead the life she was leading, and this loss is severe in the extreme. It is thus obvious why we care about the kind of personal survival the narrative self-constitution view links to identity. It is part of being a person to value living a certain kind of life and having a certain kind of experience. To the extent that we are already persons by the time we are addressing philosophical questions of personal identity, we are already creatures who value the kind of orientation toward the world that defines personal existence. The horror we feel at the prospect of losing our capacity to experience the world we do or to interact with others as persons is thus perfectly comprehensible and natural to our state.

These facts are sufficient to provide the relevant kind of explanation of survival's importance on the narrative self-constitution view. An interesting question remains, however, about whether it is possible to make a stronger claim about the value of survival—whether the narrative self-constitution view gives us a definition according to which survival is something that *should* matter to us in an absolute or categorical sense. The impetus for this question comes from the already acknowledged fact that there may be nonpersonal forms of existence that are not inferior to personhood. It seems obvious that it is less desirable to slip into senility than to continue as a person (although the clarity of even this order of preference presupposes some of the values held by persons), but what about satori or similar states? From the point of view of the Buddhist it is the misguided attachment we feel to personal survival that keeps us from true enlightenment. From this perspective survival is something to be transcended, not valued.[8]

It would be nice if there were some way to argue that personhood is absolutely the best form of existence, but it is not even clear what it would mean to provide such an argument. Values, desires, wants, and aversions are things that take place within a particular kind of existence. To justify one mode of existence over another, we would have to appeal to some system of values outside of any particular mode, and it is not at all clear what this would be like. Even if we appeal to something primitive, like biological facts (arguing, for example, that living as a person is the best means of perpetuating the survival of the human organism), we cannot get a foothold. Although personhood most likely *is* a form of psychological organization particularly conducive to biological survival, we have no argument that this kind of survival is itself particularly valuable. Indeed, many of the perspectives that would have us transcend personal survival enjoin us also to devalue biological survival. Similarly, we might try to say that personhood is, at least, the best form of existence if one is living among persons, because it allows an individual to be well-integrated into society. But again, we can advocate this integration only by appeal to values already intrinsic to personhood—for example, the ability to achieve personal goals or find personal happiness, and a perspective asking us to reject personhood might well reject the value of these as well.

Different forms of existence are, it seems, true incommensurables, and so it appears that there can be no straightforward argument that one form is

---

[8] I am indebted to my reviewer for pointing out the need for this discussion.

superior to another. Even those who would have us reject personhood usually acknowledge that doing so requires some sort of conversion experience, thus recognizing that the reasons for preferring another mode of life cannot be found within personal existence. There are, of course, various considerations that might persuade a person to see the value of another way of being, and a study of what these are and how they work would prove most interesting. What is most important to recognize here, however, is that it is not necessary for our present purposes to sort through this immensely complex issue. All that is required is to explain why we *do* care about survival, and the narrative self-constitution view is perfectly able to do that.

It might be protested, however, that the explanatory burden I have set for identity theories is now too light. If all that is required to explain the importance of survival is a descriptive account of our concern and not a normative one, psychological continuity theorists, too, are able to meet that demand. Parfit, for instance, explains our interest in survival as based on a mistake—we think that survival is a deeper fact than it turns out to be, and so we feel a misplaced concern about it. That we presuppose a mistaken metaphysics explains why we *do* value survival, although it also implies that we *should not*. To show that the narrative self-constitution view is in a significantly better position to explain the importance of identity than the psychological continuity theory, then, it is necessary to say a few words about the relevant differences between the two.

The essential difference can best be seen by recognizing that although the narrative self-constitution view does not give an *absolute* justification of the importance of survival, it does not give a purely descriptive account either. This view justifies survival's importance in terms of the most primitive values common to persons, and if these cannot be further justified it is because they are, in a real sense, primitives. The situation is quite different with the psychological continuity theory, which ultimately cannot account for the importance of identity even in terms of the values that persons actually do hold. The narrative self-constitution view, then, can explain why *persons* should care about personal survival, even though it cannot explain why *any* sentient creature should. Psychological continuity theorists, on the other hand, cannot even explain why survival should matter to *persons*.

An analogy might help to underscore this difference. If someone were to ask, for instance, why people hate breaking their legs, it would be perfectly easy to give an answer—it is very painful to break one's leg; it makes it much more difficult to get around; it interferes with daily routine, and so on. We can, of course, imagine cases where a broken leg might turn out to be a blessing in disguise, but in general the list of ill effects is enough to explain why people should be keen to avoid such an injury. If we were pressed further, however, to explain what is so bad about being in pain, or being vulnerable, or being unable to carry out one's routine, we have trouble finding anything more to say. We take it as a primitive that as a general rule these things are ills to be avoided when possible. It may be a deep and important fact that we cannot say anything further here, but it does not mean that we have failed to make sense of the fact that people value intact limbs.

The narrative self-constitution view gives an account of the importance of identity that is much like this account of the importance of whole limbs. It does take for granted some primitives that can be assumed of persons and hence only shows why survival is important to persons, not why it is important overall. Since persons really do hold the values assumed, however, and hold them not as mere conventions but as definitional aspects of their existence, showing that they justify our interest in survival is showing something quite significant.

The analogous position for psychological continuity theorists is quite different. To return to the example of the broken leg, it is as if these theorists were to claim that we are mistaken about the nature of broken legs—that it is only an elaborate hoax that has kept us believing that they are painful or debilitating. (We can imagine, for instance, that people who break their limbs aren't let in on the joke until they reach the hospital.) Now, if this turned out to be the case, we would all agree that it is hard to say what is so bad about a broken leg—just as if survival really were only psychological continuation as defined by these theorists, we would be at a loss to say what is so good about it.

The psychological continuity theory's account of the origins of our interest in identity thus rests on the view that survival is not what we thought it was and has the consequence that a reasonable person will give up that interest and find an alternative form of existence. The narrative self-constitution view maintains our conception of the nature of survival and has no such implications. It thus offers an explanation of the value of survival of a sort the psychological continuity theory is unable to give. In this way the narrative self-constitution view avoids the force of the extreme claim with respect to survival in a way that the psychological continuity theory cannot.

I turn next to the consideration of self-interested concern. The most straightforward link between the formation of an autobiographical narrative and self-interested concern can be seen by recalling that what makes a particular anticipation of the future a part of someone's narrative is precisely the influence it has on the character of his present experience. An expected future pain is included in a person's narrative when it casts a shadow over the present moment, making it less pleasurable; and an anticipated boon is incorporated when it mitigates present suffering. This is just the phenomenological effect of forming a narrative self-conception described earlier. To think about the relation of this effect to self-interested concern, one need only contrast the type of childhood sorrow George Eliot describes in saying that "there is no hopelessness so sad as that of early youth, when the soul is made up of wants, and has no long memories, no superadded life in the life of others; though we who look on think lightly of such premature despair, as if our vision of the future lightened the blind sufferer's present,"[9] with the elation of Lady Macbeth, who, having been told of the witches' prophecy for her husband, tells him, "Thy letters have transported me beyond / This ignorant present, and I feel now / The future in the instant."[10] The child who has not yet fully formed its self-conception and so does not fully appropriate its future will be less comforted in the present by its future possibilities than either the mature Lady Macbeth, who is able to live those possibilities now, or the other adults who can see the shortsightedness of the grieving child's perspective.[11]

To a certain extent, then, the narrative self-constitution view can justify concern for the future by the mere fact that what makes a future one's own on this view is that its anticipated character can cause pleasure or pain in the present. The present person thus has an obvious and immediate stake in anticipating a pleasant future. But this aspect of the narrative self-constitution view is not yet enough to capture fully our intuitions about self-interested concern. What has been said so far does not really show that a person has reason to care about the future, only about his anticipations of it. Attending only to this phenomenon, it would seem that the most reasonable course of action for a pleasure-seeking person would be to try and convince himself that his future will be wonderful no matter what the truth of the matter. Such a conviction, should he achieve it, would make his present more enjoyable. This is not, however, what our intuitions about self-interested concern tell us. We believe that people should be concerned less about the character they *expect* the future to have than about the character it *will* have. Indeed, it is considered highly imprudent to believe without

---

[9] George Eliot, *The Mill on the Floss* (New York: Penguin, 1985), p. 320.

[10] William Shakespeare, *The Tragedy of Macbeth*, 1.5.56–58.

[11] Of course, in the case of real persons the issues are more complicated. Adults can be quite childlike in their anticipations or acceptance of certain aspects of their futures, and children quite mature. For an extremely useful discussion of the vicissitudes of our relations to our own futures, see Wollheim, *The Thread of Life*, pp. 235–56.

cause that the future will be rosy. Such optimism often prevents the healthy anxiety that motivates persons to take the steps required to secure a truly enjoyable future. A person should thus have conern that her future actually *be* pleasant, not just that she now *believe* that it will be, and it remains to be explained why this is so.

It is here that the general expansionist effects of having a self-narrative once again become important. It is essential to recall that the impact of conceiving of oneself as a persisting subject with a future is quite widespread. The qualitative effects of thinking of oneself in terms of a narrative go far beyond the particular local effects described above. Not only does the anticipation of a specific future event impact in particular ways on the subjectivity of the moment at which it is anticipated, the recognition that one has a future is constantly with a person and alters *everything* about present experience.

Reconsider the George Eliot quotation. What young children lack is *perspective*. The present takes up too much space for them because they have not yet learned to view it as just one small piece of an ongoing story that will yet take many twists and turns. The capacity to take this long view is seen as a hallmark of maturity. It, too, is aptly described by Eliot when she says, "strange, that some of us, with quick alternate vision, see beyond our infatuations, and even while we rave on the heights behold the wide plain where our persistent self pauses and awaits us."[12] Thought of one's future brings more than the singular thrill or comfort of some specific anticipation; it brings the sense that there is more than just what is present at the moment, and this makes the present a wholly different kind of thing. This is just the effect described earlier by Wollheim, when he explained the two ways the phenomenology of the past and future make themselves felt in the present.

Concern for the future should thus not be conceived primarily as an event that can be localized to a particular time in a person's life—or even to a collection of different times at which there is occurrent anticipation or fear. It is an ongoing, active orientation that creates a kind of experience that is not present without it. The subject worrying about his future is a narrative self and not some particular moment of this self, so the effects of self-concern do not consist only in the fact that at one moment (or even at each moment) a particular *anticipated* future changes a person's present. Instead, the formation of a narrative brings into being a temporally extended subject who has this concern for her whole self. By the time someone is in

[12]George Eliot, *Middlemarch* (New York: Penguin, 1985), p. 182.

the position to worry about the future he is already more than a momentary creature.

The feature of autobiographical narrative to which I am pointing is the one we have discussed repeatedly. Formation of a narrative creates a persisting subject who is conceptually prior to its temporal parts. This subject clearly has an interest not only in the quality of the present moment, but in that of the narrative as a whole. At each moment the possessor of an autobiographical narrative is claiming the whole story to be *her* story, and a story with a happy ending is generally more desirable than a story with a sad one.[13] We can thus see that the narrative self-constitution view explains not just why a person is justifiably concerned about the anticipated character of his future, but about the future itself.

Having seen how the narrative self-constitution view provides a basis for self-interested concern, a similar argument for compensation follows quickly. The concept of compensation is closely tied to that of self-interested concern—it is because we care about what our futures will be like that the promise of forthcoming benefits can make up for present difficulties. The same features that make self-interested concern appropriate thus justify our practices of compensation. First, it is the case that the anticipation of compensation can actually lighten a person's burden in the present. The knowledge that today's hard work will be rewarded tomorrow can make the suffering easier to bear, and so compensation can occur in the present as well as the future. More important, however, the formation of an autobiographical self-conception creates a persisting subject who is, as I have argued, appropriately concerned for the whole of her life story. Because of this, a happy outcome can reasonably be taken to compensate for a rough patch. The story in which someone suffers an injustice and then is restored to her rightful position, for instance, is a happier story than one in which right never prevails, as the story in which someone works diligently and is well rewarded is a happier one than that of a life of unmitigated drudgery. Since the relevant subject has a legitimate and primary concern with her narrative as a whole, our practices and attitudes surrounding compensation are thus supported by the narrative self-constitution view as well.

All that remains is to discuss how the narrative self-constitution view explains the intuitive relation between moral responsibility and identity. Before beginning this discussion it is important to acknowledge that issues

---

[13]This is meant as a general observation. It is, of course, possible to prefer the life of a tragically misunderstood artist or antihero to one defined by common happiness. More generally, we can say that a life more to one's taste is preferable to one which is not, and that the ending of the story is relevant to determining whether or not one's life is to one's taste.

of moral responsibility are extremely complex. It is not clear that a person is to be held responsible for *all* of her actions, nor even that she can never be held responsible in any way for actions that are not hers. I cannot address the trickier questions of moral responsibility here. My interest is in our very powerful sense that the question of whether a person took some particular action is, to say the very least, deeply relevant to the question of whether she is to be held responsible for it. So although it may be that the set of actions for which a person is responsible is not exactly coextensive with the set of actions that are hers, there will be considerable overlap, and it is this fact which the narrative self-constitution view is charged with explaining.

There are two aspects of the view relevant to this particular task. The first is the one that has been playing a prominent role throughout our discussion—the capacity of this view to allow for a deep link between the different temporal portions of a person's life. This is important because one part of the connection between personal identity and moral responsibility has to do with issues surrounding the justice of punishment. Punishment is unpleasant, and we feel that it is fair for a subject to experience the unpleasantness consequent on an ill deed only if he is, in fact, the same subject who committed it. The psychological continuity theory's inability to provide unity of consciousness over time thus makes basing punishment on identity (as that view defines it) seem unfair. Punishment can in fact be seen as the flip side of compensation. Whereas it seems right to reward virtuous action with something that is pleasant to the virtuous subject, it also seems right to detract from the ill-gotten pleasures of the vicious subject.

To the extent that it is this aspect of moral responsibility which is at issue, our earlier discussion of how the narrative self-constitution view justifies self-concern and compensation can be applied without much alteration. Since the relevant unit of concern on this view is the narrative as a whole, and since a person has an interest in the character of the whole of her life story, it makes sense that just punishment must take questions of identity into account. On the narrative self-constitution view, saying that the person who committed the crime is the one who is punished for it is saying that the crime and punishment occur in the same narrative. To the extent that the punishment affects the overall narrative, then, it affects the subject who took the action, and the worries of the extreme claim are avoided.

Punishment is not, however, the only aspect of the link between moral responsibility and personal identity—agency is also an issue. In order to be held morally responsible at all, one must be a moral agent, and in order to be held responsible for a particular action one must have agency with respect to it. It is thus taken for granted that there is a link between agency and personal identity—persons have more control over their own actions than those of others. Although there are many thorny issues about agency that cannot be settled here, I think it is fairly easy to see how identity as defined by the narrative self-constitution view is connected to agency. This is true both at the most general level of the connection between being a person and being an agent, and at the more particular level of the connection between a specific action being one's own and one having agency with respect to that action.

At the general level, we can see that a person needs a narrative self-conception in order to be an agent at all. Without the sense of oneself as a persisting individual whose actions should cohere with one's beliefs, values, and desires (which should also cohere with one another) and whose current actions have implications for the future, one does not have the capacity for moral responsibility. We do not hold infants, the insane, or sufferers from dementia responsible for their actions as we do typical adults. Their inability to see their lives unfolding in an intelligible manner—to make their actions, experiences, beliefs, and desires cohere—leaves these people incapable of making the kinds of decisions necessary to agency. The kind of psychological organization that makes an individual a person on the narrative self-constitution view is thus precisely the kind required for being an agent.

At a more specific level, we can see that the inclusion of a particular action in a person's self-narrative situates it in his life in such a way that he has agency with respect to it. What it means for an action to be part of someone's narrative is for it to flow naturally from the rest of her life story—to be an intelligible result of her beliefs, values, desires, and experiences, and although it may not be the case that an action must *always* have this kind of relation to the rest of a person's life in order for him to have agency with respect to it, these features are certainly generally considered part of what determines the degree of moral responsibility assigned. The more an action seems to stem from a coherent and stable pattern of values, desires, goals, and character traits, the more it seems under a person's control. When a person's action is anomalous or inexplicable in terms of the rest of her experience and psyche, it seems less likely that the impetus for it comes from her—a point Frankfurt, among others, has emphasized. The greater the anomaly the more we suspect that the source of the action is somehow external to the person in a way relevant to mitigating her agency and hence her responsibility. Although issues of moral responsibility are extremely complex, then, it is clear that both in terms of issues of the justice of punishment and questions of agency, the narrative self-constitution view captures our intuitions concerning the intimate link between identity and moral responsibility.

It is thus possible to see a connection between personal identity as defined by the narrative self-constitution view and each of the four features. The fundamental element underlying all four connections is the person as a persisting subject of experience. A narrative subject is not only *affected* by the past and future, she *experiences* them, and this makes the practices and attitudes that define her life not only possible but natural. It is no accident that the rehumanization of Ebenezer Scrooge—the change that allows him to once again become part of personal intercourse—comes from his being forced to acknowledge and experience not only his present but also his past and future. When his cure is finally achieved, he expresses the lesson he has learned by telling the spirit of Christmas-yet-to-come "I will live in the Past, Present, and the Future. The Spirits of all Three shall strive within me."[14] It is this kind of temporally extended life which creates persons, and which makes the four features part of our lives. It comes from recognizing oneself as the appropriate sort of narrative subject.

Our concerns about persons are enormously complex, and persons themselves even more so. No philosophical account of persons can be complete without acknowledging that persons as we know them are almost always human beings, and that they almost always live together in highly organized social groups; that persons and their customs can vary a great deal, and that we evolve psychologically and socially as well as physically; that mortality is a fact of our lives; that sometimes we need to think of other persons as mere objects or biological machines, whereas at other times it is essential to think of them as transcending biology and the natural order.

  Given the diversity of personal existence, it should not be expected that a single theory can speak to all of our concerns. This does not mean, of course, that there should be no attempt to integrate our various perspectives on persons. No *one* account can capture all of our interests, but that does not mean that the set of accounts speaking to different questions of personhood and personal identity should be viewed as totally independent of one another. Our concepts of persons and their identities may not, in the end, be *totally* consistent, but there should at least be a general coherence and thematic unity among them that makes them all theories of persons. The way to find this coherence, however, is not to try and force all of our

[14]Charles Dickens, *A Christmas Carol* (Toronto: Bantam, 1986), pp. 79-80.

intuitions about personhood and personal identity into a single mold, but rather to develop each set of insights and concerns on its own terms and consider the relations among them afterward.

The argument of this book provides a clear and compelling example of the value of this approach. Psychological continuity theorists run into trouble because they try to do too much at once. They expect a single account of personal identity both to answer the reidentification question and to illuminate the connection between identity and the four features. This expectation, we have seen, leads them to develop a view that fails to attain either goal. I have argued that the ultimate problem for psychological continuity theorists is their failure to distinguish between different aspects of our concern with persons and their identities, and to recognize that the question of identity that is relevant to the four features is not the reidentification question.

Acknowledging the differences between the characterization and reidentification questions has allowed us to recognize the characterization question as the appropriate context in which to investigate the relation between personal identity and the four features. Consideration of this question on its own terms led to the development of the narrative self-constitution view. Free from the restrictions of logical form associated with the reidentification question, this view is able to define identity in such a way that it entails a deeply unified and persisting subject of experience. The existence of such a subject in turn makes sense of our attitudes and practices surrounding the four features. Moreover, once the details of the narrative self-constitution view are spelled out, we are able to see how issues of characterization are connected to issues of reidentification, and hence to see how the narrative self-constitution view defines identity in a way that respects and incorporates our intuitions about the importance of bodily identity to personal identity—something psychological continuity theorists cannot do.

Separating the investigation of the relation between personal identity and the four features from the project of defining a reidentification criterion for persons thus resolves many of the tensions and inconsistencies that plague psychological continuity theorists, and in the end provides a much clearer picture of how a bewildering variety of intuitions about personal identity can ultimately be integrated and reconciled. This work already pushes the philosophical discussion of personal identity forward a great deal, and there is every reason to hope that a continuing sensitivity to the many different kinds of questions and concerns we have surrounding persons and their identities will continue to bear fruit. The Delphic injunction plays a prominent role in the history of human thought, but the task it sets is ambiguous. Knowing ourselves involves a great many different kinds of activities, and we should not rest content with any one. It is easy to conflate the astonishingly complicated sets of issues surrounding personhood and personal identity, and it is tempting to oversimplify them. There is, however, a great deal to be gained by appreciating the intricacies of ourselves and our lives and pushing forward through the thicket.

Selected Bibliography

Bruner, Jerome. *Acts of Meaning*. Cambridge: Harvard University Press, 1990.

——. *Actual Minds/Possible Worlds*. Cambridge: Harvard University Press, 1986.

Butler, Joseph. "Of Personal Identity." In J. Perry, ed., *Personal Identity*. Berkeley and Los Angeles: University of California Press, 1976.

Carter, William R. "Why Personal Identity Is Animal Identity." *LOGOS: Philosophic Issues in Christian Perspective* 11 (1990).

Dennett, Daniel. *Elbow Room: The Varieties of Free Will Worth Wanting*. Cambridge: MIT Press, 1990.

Frankfurt, Harry. "Freedom of the Will and the Concept of a Person." In Gary Watson, ed., *Free Will*. Oxford: Oxford University Press, 1983.

——. "Identification and Externality." In A. Rorty, ed., *The Identities of Persons*. Berkeley and Los Angeles: University of California Press, 1976.

Freeman, Mark. *Rewriting the Self: History, Memory, Narrative*. London: Routledge, 1993.

Glover, Jonathan. *The Philosophy and Psychology of Personal Identity*. London: Penguin, 1988.

James, William. *The Principles of Psychology*. Vol. 1. New York: Dover, 1950.

Kramer, Peter D. *Listening to Prozac: A Psychiatrist Explores Antidepressant Drugs and the Remaking of the Self*. New York: Viking, 1993.

Lahav, Ran. "What Neuropsychology Tells Us about Consciousness." *Philosophy of Science* 60, no. 1 (March 1993): 70.

Lewis, David. *Philosophical Papers*. Vol. 1. Oxford: Oxford University Press, 1983.

Locke, John. *An Essay concerning Human Understanding*. Ed. P. Nidditch. Oxford: Clarendon Press, 1979.

MacIntyre, Alasdair. "The Virtues, the Unity of a Human Life, and the Concept of a Tradition." In Stanley Hauerwas and L. Gregory Jones, eds., *Why Narrative?* Grand Rapids, Mich.: Wm. B. Eerdmans, 1989.

Noonan, Harold. *Personal Identity*. London: Routledge, 1991.

Nozick, Robert. *Philosophical Explanations*. Oxford: Clarendon Press, 1981.

Parfit, Derek. *Reasons and Persons*. Oxford: Clarendon Press, 1984.

Perry, John. "Can the Self Divide?" *The Journal of Philosophy* 69 no. 16 (September 7, 1972).

——. "The Importance of Being Identical." In A. Rorty, ed., *The Identities of Persons*. Berkeley and Los Angeles: University of California Press, 1976.

——, ed. *Personal Identity*. Berkeley and Los Angeles: University of California Press, 1976.

Polonoff, David. "Self-Deception." *Social Research* 54 (1987).

Reid, Thomas. "Of Mr. Locke's Account of Our Personal Identity." In J. Perry, ed., *Personal Identity*. Berkeley and Los Angeles: University of California Press, 1976.

Sartre, Jean-Paul. *Being and Nothingness*. New York: Washington Square Press, 1956.

Schafer, Roy. "Narration in the Psychoanalytic Dialogue." In W.J.T. Mitchell, ed., *On Narrative*. Chicago: University of Chicago Press, 1981.

Shoemaker, Sydney. "A Materialist's Account." In Shoemaker and Richard Swinburne, *Personal Identity*. Oxford: Blackwell, 1984.

Spence, Donald. *Narrative Truth and Historical Truth*. New York: W. W. Norton, 1982.

Taylor, Charles. "Responsibility for the Self." In Gary Watson, ed., *Free Will*. Oxford: Oxford University Press, 1983.

Whiting, Jennifer. "Friends and Future Selves." *Philosophical Review* 95, no. 4 (October 1986).

Williams, Bernard. "The Self and the Future." In J. Perry, ed., *Personal Identity*. Berkeley and Los Angeles: University of California Press, 1976.

Wollheim, Richard. *The Thread of Life*, Cambridge: Harvard University Press, 1984.

Index

Action
  and moral responsibility, 80–81, 158
  and person, 106–7, 109, 117, 133
  theory of, 75
Agency, 158–59
Ancestral relation, 28, 30, 55–56, 62
Anticipation, 57, 62–63, 154–57
Articulation constraint, 114–19, 130
  and attribution, 117–19
  and self-narrative, 115–16
Attribution, 90–92, 133, 149
  and articulation, 117–19
  of characteristics, 76–77
  and degree, 79–80
  and four features, 91–92
  and sameness of consciousness, 136
Augustine, 113

Barclay, Craig, 124–25
Blindsight, 139–40
Bodily continuity theory, 13, 15, 21, 67–70
  and narrative self-constitution view, 120,
    130–34
  and subjectivity, 69
Brain, 22–25, 60–61, 147–48, 150
Bruner, Jerome, 96
Buddhist view, 100–101, 152
Butler, Joseph, 52, 54

Carter, William R., 56
Characterization question, 1–2, 68–70
  and attribution, 76–77
  basic form of, 74–76
  and degree, 79
  and extreme claim, 89–91, 136
  and four features, 2–3, 69–70, 78
  as Lockean, 106n

  and person-stages, 77, 91
  and self-interested concern, 85
  and transitivity objection, 79
  and true identity, 73–74
Co-consciousness, 137–42
  See also Consciousness
Coherence, 98
Compensation, 2, 14
  and consciousness, 157
  degree of, 86
  and extreme claim, 56
  and qualitative similarity, 52–53
Connectedness
  direct, 20, 28
  strong, 20, 28–30, 43–44
Consciousness, 53–54
  affective side of, 108–9
  backward extension of, 106–10
  and co-consciousness, 137–42
  and compensation, 157
  degree of, 141, 148
  and experiencing subject, 61
  and four features, 149–60
  and implicit knowledge, 139–40
  influences on, 110–12, 139–42
  loss of, 87–88, 147–48, 150–52
  and moral responsibility, 157–60
  and nonconsciousness, 140–42
  quality of, 144
  reidentification of, 142
  sameness of, 19, 27, 106–7, 136–42, 149–
    60
  sameness of over time, 142–49
  and self-conception, 116
  and self-interested concern, 154–57
  as shared knowledge, 107–8
  and survival, 87–88, 150–54

Printed in the United States
134838LV00010B/10/A